THE TELEVISION MEDIA PARADIGM

Pendulums of Power – Volume I

René Normandeau

Published by: René Normandeau

DISCLAIMER

All events mentioned in this book are simply memories that have been transcribed to the accuracy of my recollection of these events, and should be regarded as such. They are not meant to be used as evidence of any kind, for any purpose.

The informational aspects are substantiated through verifiable references which are presented to support a philosophy of inquiry. They are not meant to convince the reader of any ideological convictions.

It is my intention to simply offer alternative ideas to accepted doctrines. I leave it to the reader to determine its merit and authenticity.

This author claims no liability or responsibility for the accuracy, or the integrity of any source provided, or the accuracy of any information, recollections or transcriptions therein, and hereby disclaims any liability to any party for any loss, damage, or disruption caused by any information, errors or omissions, whether such information, errors or omissions result from negligence, accident, or any other cause.

Note: Certain references to the Queen of England may be substituted for King Charles, where appropriate.

To my children and grand-children. May knowledge forever remain uncensored to your eyes, and light the path to wisdom

TABLE OF CONTENTS

PREFACE

In August of 1991, a British computer scientist working at CERN Laboratories in Geneva Switzerland, introduced the World Wide Web to humankind, marking the beginning of the age of information, where anyone could share their knowledge in an open forum of expression and communication.

Staged amongst this landmark event, was the launching of my career in the world of media, where I was first employed by the Canadian Broadcasting Corporation (CBC), following my post-graduate studies in audio engineering at the Ontario Institute of Audio Recording Technology in London, Ontario, Canada.

This is the story of my twenty-five-year journey in the media and entertainment industries, and my lifelong path of exploration into the inner mechanisms of the reality in which we exist.

It is an eye-witness account of the world of media, as observed through the eyes of a television technician, researcher and investigator.

It is an attempt to clarify the mis-conceptions associated with media and journalism.

It is a challenge to our beliefs and perceptions of truth.

It is an inquisitive look into the world of government and big brother.

It is a look at ourselves.

It is the platform I have chosen to expose information that I feel should be known by everyone.

It is an honest and un-censored transcript of the relevant experiences of my journey.

Although my insights and perspectives are centered around my experiences working at the CBC, the policies and formatting of local news programs are very similar throughout the world.

I encourage the reader to further expand upon the information and ideologies presented, as they are meant simply as a doorway to open minded conversation and exploration of this boundless existence, beyond the rigidly confined parameters of conventional societal dogma.

INTRODUCTION

Most of us would not recall a man named Philo Farnsworth. In 1927, he filed a patent for a device that he invented dubbed the *"image dissector"*, a vacuum tube used in video cameras and monitors. He was the first to develop a fully functioning, all-electric television system, and was also responsible for the invention of the cathode ray tube used to project the images onto a screen.

Although film and audio tape were the standard platforms in the early stages of television broadcasting, by 1991, when I began my career in media, the choice medium had evolved to broadcast quality analog Beta video tape, where video and audio could be recorded and edited together on a single platform.

This analog technology, with respect to studio applications, required a human presence at every technical position.

The studio crew consisted of a video switcher, audio operator, font operator, teleprompter operator, director, production assistant (PA), studio camera operators, studio assistant, VTR operator and on camera personalities. The director ran the show and the PA assured adherence to the precisely calculated timeline.

All visual material and items were compiled by video editors, and subsequently delivered to a VTR suite consisting of three playback machines, from where all of the show's content were aired.

Producing a live television news program is not for the faint of heart. It was not uncommon to see new employees walk out of the studio in tears after a show with a particularly harsh director.

It's a back-and-forth frenzy of live mixing. Let us listen in on the studio chatter from the first few minutes of a live news broadcast and familiarize ourselves with the background madness associated with a typical newscast, as it was done back in the '90's.

Crew Member Designations: **Producer**, *Production Assistant*, **Audio Technician**, Remote Location Tech, <u>Studio Assistant</u>, *<u>Teleprompter Operator</u>*, **Studio Eleven Editor**, ***Studio Camera Operator***, *<u>Switcher</u>*… (reference to forty-nine is the studio control room designation)

"*We are live on the air in five…four…**roll VTR**…two…one…**take VTR now…camera one ready…take camera one now…camera one zoom in**…cue…font…we are going to VTR A for a voice over…take VTR in three…**roll VTR…remote can you hear me…take VTR…test one two**…we hear you forty-nine…**I'm not getting their audio**…**remote we're not hearing you**…hold on I'll check…coming out of this in three…**go to camera one now**…we are rolling VTR B in three…**roll VTR…take VTR now**…remote, forty-nine…yeah we should be good for audio now…**yep got it…audio's good**…yeah the battery just died…one minute to end of item…**we are going to camera two, then two boards, get ready camera two…zoom in a little bit…ok good**…<u>host wants the teleprompter to slow down</u>…**teleprompter**…yeah I heard him…out of this in three…two…**take camera two now…are these guys done yet…studio eleven, forty-nine…<u>almost done…putting on the last shot now</u>**…ok you're next…three* *twenty…***you've got three minutes***…<u>camera two can you check your focus please</u>…***oops yeah sorry…is that good***…<u>yeah much better</u>…***ready board one…take one…two…back to camera two…now***…*going to VTR C in…three…***roll VTR***…*two…***take VTR***…**eleven I need an answer, you guys gonna be ready…you're coming up…**<u>**yeah going to VTR now**</u>…**ok thanks**…<u>*remote can you do a white balance please*</u>…*one minute to end of item*…**ok we are going to camera one…camera two give me a two shot…we are going to camera one for a voice over then to camera two…camera three head and shoulders**…<u>weather says she can barely hear you</u>…**tell her to turn the volume up on her telex**…**the one on the cord**…<u>ok it's better now</u>…*<u>that's better remote</u>*…*out of this in three…two*…**take camera one now**…*ready camera two*…**camera two…MIC!!!** <u>MIC!!!</u> MIC!!!…***font her…***sorry…*going to VTR A*…***take VTR***…"*

A "gong show" is what the PA used to call it, referring mostly to occasions where the scene could become quite heated as problems arose and machinery malfunctioned.

Sadly, advancements in technology and robotics have allowed the entire production to be reduced to a two-person crew consisting of simply a switcher and director.

Through the emergence of digital technology, also arose the age of the internet, and I suddenly found myself sitting in front of a laptop connected to the world wide web.

The wealth of information offered by this powerful tool now at my disposal, prompted my decision to retire my mind from television zombification, and enter the world of internet re-education. As the available content grew, so did my interests, and it led me down a path of discovery, allowing me to unearth a hidden wealth of knowledge, from a world that was to me, hitherto unknown, and helped me to uncover the secrets concealing the true objectives of media.

Chapter 1

STRUCTURE AND CONTROL

The media is a very regulated and structured environment. Its far-reaching influence requires strict adherence to well established policies, intended to assure that its resources are not exploited for nefarious purposes.

Although we can understand the need to restrict the distribution of sensitive information that could be harmful to certain groups or individuals, we must still uphold the fundamental principles required to ensure that our public servants are held accountable to their constituents.

This responsibility also extends to the governing bodies which control its programming. A state-owned media for example, can be utilized as a tool of oppression. Freedom of the press is therefore paramount to the security of any society, and must be safeguarded with utmost vigilance.

Defining the parameters that separate slander from liability obligations can be a challenging endeavor that is made especially difficult in a climate of social insecurity.

In such circumstances, the ability to properly render a fair and balanced reportage becomes significantly reduced and allows for a rise in corruption, as important facts can be sheltered behind socially unacceptable boundaries.

We may not be able to address the influx of immigrants for example, as this subject might raise issues of discrimination.

In extreme conditions, the political establishment may take advantage of these societal limits to operate beyond the sphere of public accountability and become the directors of published information.

The control of media however, is accomplished through several methods, and it begins with the manner in which televised news programs are structured.

Local newscasts are pressured by the restrictive timeframes imposed upon them by the industry standard of daily broadcasts.

For this purpose, a set of routines governed by strict policies have been established to permit such an industry to effectively deliver their product on a daily basis.

Gathering information with great efficiency is paramount, and there are a number of predictable daily events which can be used to fill the allotted time on air. This information is strictly managed through the corporate policies which state that the newscast will consist of stories relating to Sports, Culture, Arts and Entertainment, Weather, Local and International News.

Let us dissect these subjects…

Culture – People, places, food, festivals, tradition. Promotes belonging in groups.

Arts and Entertainment – Painting, drawing, writing, movies, theater, festivals etc. promotes lifestyle.

Sports – Running, driving, riding, jumping, swimming, diving, kicking, shooting, physical violence and games. Gives you the sensation that you are a part of something… part of a team. A form of entertainment which provides a sense of inclusion. A form of distraction.

Weather – Weather predictions and anomalies. Creates comfort and also instigates fear.

Local and International news – Accidents, local political activity, elections, house fires, thefts, murders, suicides, beatings and a plethora of other things related to daily life, as well as international events such as wars, conflicts, economic activity, shootings, political affairs etc.

We are led to believe that the content outlined by these policies and its method of delivery is indicative of an efficient and modern form of communication, essential to a well-informed public. The fact is however, that the media was not structured in a manner in which to accommodate a "well-informed" public.

Not only is information filtered through this list of policies, but this fast paced, news on demand brand of reporting does not allow for any in-depth research or analysis to be conducted on any subject, therefore pressuring news organizations to rely on sources that they must presume trustworthy.

This constant need to accommodate the media, led to the creation of press releases and press conferences.

The Press Release

Press releases are routinely used by governments, businesses, and various organizations, to convey newsworthy information to the public. Most now include on their websites, a press release section that is accessible to the media, or anyone interested in their respective activities.

Various levels of government will often fax press releases directly to news agencies to convey important information, and to assure a media presence at press conferences.

Journalists have become so accustomed to receiving these faxes, that browsing through the press release section of government websites is not even considered.

This enables politicians to selectively communicate information to the public, while remaining somewhat transparent, as information that they do not want publicized on the news are effectively concealed in plain sight on their website, insightful of the fact that most will not venture to read these publications.

Politicians will not readily make themselves available for interviews to discuss such unpopular topics, but will openly host press conferences regarding less threatening subject that they do want publicized, generating a consistent public presence, whilst facilitating media coverage with accessible video and audio content.

Although the press conference is a valuable tool for both media and government, its objectives might not be as forthcoming as expected.

Once a more open and transparent platform, todays press conference has become a controlled environment where journalists and their questions are vetted by the government, and in certain situations, the politicians involved will not even entertain questions from the press.

Naturally, smaller local events… such as the opening of a new youth center… do not merit such censorship, but more impactful federal matters will assuredly engender such actions.

The following is an example of such instances where our elected officials operate above public accountability, and the media, neglecting their responsibilities to hold these public servants accountable, are instead reduced to glamorizing the event as a means to impersonate news coverage.

FLASHBACK…

There was an occasion where newly elected, US President Obama, visited Canada's capital, Ottawa. It was a media frenzy. One media organization in particular… the one I worked for… was offering full, non-stop coverage of the event. They had reporters stationed at all possible venues where the President and his entourage were likely to make an appearance. We saw a glimpse of the President as he debarked from his aircraft. We then cut to analysts discussing the event. We saw a glimpse of the President as he walked by the windows of the legislative building on his tour of the edifice, alongside Prime Minister Harper. We then heard back from the analysts who were offering their opinions on what the two leaders would be discussing at their meeting. Trade and relations were among the topics. We were shown footage of adoring fans gathered around the compound, desperate to get a glimpse of their mentor.

The moment of truth finally arrived, as our fearless leaders stepped out of the legislative building for the scheduled press conference. Looking visibly satisfied, Harper and Obama proceeded to inform us that the President felt welcome in our country and that they did indeed discuss trade and relations… before quickly re-disappearing back into the legislative building. We then cut back to the analysts bragging that their predictions had indeed been correct.

But it wasn't over yet. The President was subsequently led to a famous and popular strip in the city, where he was introduced to a popular local treat named "beavertails". By coincidence, the journalist stationed back at the airport lived in that particular area of the city and was quite familiar with its local shops and delicacies. Considering the fact that she had been stuck at the airport missing all the action, the producers felt that it was a good opportunity to give her some airtime and take advantage of her familiarity with this special treat to enlighten their viewers. As they cut to her, she purposefully made it quite obvious that she was visibly disgruntled at the fact that she had been stuck at the airport all day, away from all the action, and further expressed her discontent at the fact that she had just lost her background of the President's jet because it was relocated a short moment before cutting to her. She proceeded to tell us all about the beavertails, and that if she were there at the moment, she would invite the president back to her place for some tea.

It was an embarrassing spectacle of un-professionalism, and a fitting tribute to the new climate of idol worshipping being perpetuated throughout the industry.

A newly elected President of the most powerful nation in the world, on his first official visit to a foreign country, is greeted by hordes of adoring fans and treated like he is a "superstar", instead of a public servant. And this "superstar" status is proliferated by news agencies who are forced to cover the event from the sidelines, and being kept completely in the dark from any discussions between the two leaders, must resort to hype and meaningless stories of beavertails, rather than reporting on the fact that the President and our Prime Minister are having meetings behind closed doors, and not a single detail is being shared with the public they serve. Furthermore, the journalists at the press conference were not allowed to ask a single question.

(End of Flashback)

The true function of the press conference should be to uphold governmental transparency. It should not be used as a red-carpet platform to elevate politicians to the status of "stars" that are beyond the reach of accountability.

Understandably, certain situations do merit discretion, and particular facts should not be released to the public... such as the names of persons who have passed away in an accident and the next of kin have yet to be informed of the tragedy... for example.

In times of war, we would not want to disclose secret military operations and expose them to our presumed enemy.

The information and access extended to international correspondents stationed in war zones therefore, are strictly regulated by the military. Nothing you see at home on the news is broadcast without first being cleared through proper government and military channels.

Cameramen and journalists are certainly not allowed to freely roam the countryside of an occupied territory. A touching human interest story, stem from the enemy's side, could potentially diminish public support for the war.

The nature of the video footage allowed to leave the country is regulated by the military, and virtually all of the information that reporters are able to gather for their stories stem from the daily press conference.

Although we can understand the need for secrecy in certain areas of military operations, the abuse of this power to control information completely stifles transparency and can be used to sway public opinion.

Contrary to the frequent grandiose depictions of news reporters in Hollywood movies, the truth is that journalists do not live in a world of accessibility. Police, government, military, corporations or secret organizations have no interest in being accountable to the media. Hence, any information which must be presented to the public is cause for careful scrutinization of its content.

Should we not question these practices? Can we truly believe ourselves to be informed by the "news", when the information we receive is filtered, edited and censored by the very organizations that should, presumably be scrutinized and exposed by the media?

If you believe to be informed because you watch the news, and never question its authenticity or truthfulness, television can become a very powerful tool indeed, to the people who control its programming.

FLASHBACK…

I was chatting with a co-worker in the newsroom one day, and watched as the fax machine rang with an incoming message. The print was quickly brought to the editor's attention, which promptly passed it along to the host of the show, who wrote a voice-over on the subject for the evening news.

I checked in on this story and realized that it was a press release from the Federal government regarding a tour being given across the country in reaction to bad publicity regarding thimerosal in flu vaccinations. The tour was entirely sponsored by the pharmaceutical companies delivering the vaccines.

I approached the subject of Government complicity in regard to the concealment of the dangers associated with thimerosal in vaccines, to a seasoned radio journalist… and once she realized that what I was suggesting was too much for her to digest, she lashed out in a "how dare you" kind of way… "you're talking about the Federal Government here!!" and quickly ended our conversation.

So, I went down to the main floor where a nurse was administering free vaccinations to all the employees, and asked her if there was thimerosal in the vaccines that she was injecting in people's blood stream. She didn't know.

"Do you have a list of ingredients", I asked her. She didn't know.

"Do you have the box that it came in" I asked. She did find the box, and upon closer examination, confirmed that it was indeed listed as one of the ingredients. The nurse was surprised at her discovery at first… until I informed her that the product is actually toxic mercury. Suddenly realizing that she was injecting poison into everyone's veins, she lashed out in a "how dare you" kind of way… "you're talking about the Federal Government here!!" and quickly ended our conversation.

I did however, manage to convince the host of the evening news to add a note at the end of the voice-over, exposing this conflict of interest.

(End of Flashback)

In essence, the federal government sent a fax to our station, and it went directly on air virtually unverified. The reason? Because every fax we receive from the federal or provincial government is automatically deemed to be truthful and factual information, as it is a designated source of "reliable information" utilized to meet daily deadlines.

I have found that most journalists worth their mettle will eventually come to recognize the crippling limitations forced upon them by such time constraints.

There are however, certain journalists that are placed in positions where they are allocated enough time to properly research their stories. These are usually limited to human interest stories, criminal investigations such as theft and fraud, environmental issues and technology. They are usually on the national payroll and all of their stories must be vetted by the national board.

I have on many occasions made suggestions to these national reporters regarding certain subjects which I felt deserved coverage, some of which were considered, but all of which were rejected by the board.

In actuality, the content and structure of any local news program is carefully designed to ensure that no "real" journalism ever emerges.

What is "real" journalism?

In order to answer that question, we must first define the word "news", as it pertains to publicly owned television news broadcasters.

"Important, relevant, well researched and unbiased information, uninfluenced by bribery, coercion, policy or dogma, that is crucial to the safety and well-being of a people and its country in protecting itself from any local or outside threats, including (and especially) its government."

You will not find this definition in the Merriam Webster or Thesaurus. However, this definition acknowledges the most important factor in the equation… the people it should serve.

Why is this definition more respectful? Because most who watch the news believe that they are being informed by a responsible media, and this definition is conducive to these beliefs. The media after all, does promote their news programs as "news you can trust" or "the most trusted". Shouldn't we hold them accountable to their promotional rhetoric?

"Real" journalism therefore, can be defined as follows…

"The gathering and presentation of well researched and unbiased information, uninfluenced by bribery, coercion, policy or dogma, that is crucial to the safety and well-being of the public it serves, in protecting itself from any local or outside threats, including (and especially) its government."

Of course, everything has its place, and the goal here is not to diminish the relevance and importance of our daily news content. However, most of the information that is congruent with our list of policies does not fall into this newly established definition of what is "news", and therefore should not belong in a "news" program.

Should we believe that the following example be considered newsworthy information, important to our safety and well-being?

A local story of a teenage girl who wanted to wear her pajama pants while attending high school, was actually picked up by the national news. The flagship news program of the entire country, trusted by the general public, and charged with the very important role of informing the population of worldly events, wars, conflicts, economic activity, government corruption etc., apparently came to the conclusion that children wearing pajama pants at school was a subject worthy of being distributed across the entire country.

Of course, the technicalities of high school dress codes might have a place on campus radio, however, the validity of airing such content on our local and national news programs must be questioned.

Television news programs have a magical ability of being able to mislead its audience into believing the mundane to be important.

Its structure is deliberately designed to create the following results:

Instill fear – Survival instincts are often induced by fear. Therefore, anything that is fearful is immediately classified as important in our brain and will garnish our full attention. We are bombarded with terrifying subjects such as wars, terrorism, economic disasters, natural disasters, theft, scams, personal security threats, murders, accidents, diseases, as well as more mundane subjects such as weather phenomena, change in routine, and even fear of your favorite sports team losing the game. Language, voice tonality, music and editing tricks are carefully chosen for dramatic effect and to elicit an emotional response.

Create apathy towards serious subjects – A news program gives you a brief overview of many subjects. It usually starts with local news, then skips to international news, arts and entertainment, weather and sports. We can be transmitting reports of our children being murdered in oversees wars, and immediately move on to a touching human interest story, then on to the weather forecast and sports coverage. Amalgamating such a diverse range of topics into one newscast composed of short overviews of diverse subjects, does not allow the brain to properly assess the content of one subject, before it is quickly abandoned for another. It is an emotional roller coaster ride that creates a dis-connect between reality and the viewing audience to the point where it breaches the differences between important and un-important. Serious subjects are intermingled with non-threatening stories of games and entertainment, and meld together to form one short news "episode". Information is then transformed into segments of a show where you get to choose which parts you like or dislike, and rather than seeing the importance of one subject over another, you simply dissect it into parts of the same show.

Destroys attention span – As children's programming is meant to destroy our attention span, the news program, as it skips from subject to subject in brief overviews, is meant to create the same effect. Our minds have become so accustomed to this fast paced, quick service, immediate gratification societal construct, that we do not take the time to truly understand or research anything. We are so trusting of the establishment, that asking questions is not even considered necessary… and occasionally portrayed as dangerous.

Create concern towards un-important subjects – Since there is so little information transcribed in a short news item, it is easy to dismiss that which you do not understand. Therefore, when we are presented with a subject which is quite easily understood… such as our favorite team being one game away from losing the play-offs, we become concerned with the things that we can understand, and disregard those which we cannot comprehend, which leads to a distorted sense of priority.

Create confusion – Due to the lack of informational content regarding any important subject, it is impossible to understand why things happen in certain ways, and you are left questioning the world and fabricating conclusions which you convince yourself as being sensible, but in reality, is simply the brain's way of making sense of nonsense.

The human psyche perceives any knowledge which is widely held as true amongst the majority of the populace, to be factual. Evidence is inconsequential. It is proof by popular belief, and used as a safety net in human interaction and communication.

We all have our opinions, but take the opinion of one, present it on the news, and this viewpoint will subsequently become known by everyone watching the show. As this viewpoint is shared and repeated, it becomes common knowledge and eventually accepted as a fact, regardless of its merit or verity.

Most of us are already aware of media censorship and control, however, the extent to which this is utilized is vastly unknown, as its purpose is hidden within a larger agenda.

The CBC is meant to operate independently from the Federal government, yet it is a Federally controlled, publicly funded corporation governed by the "Broadcasting Act". Since we all know that a state-controlled media is anathema to a free society, we are led to believe that the CBC operates autonomously, and therefore secures its position as a government watchdog on a free and independent media platform.

Broadcasting Act[1]

46 (5) Independence

"The Corporation shall, in the pursuit of its objects and in the exercise of its powers, enjoy freedom of expression and journalistic, creative and programming independence."

However, it further states that...

47 (1)

"Except as provided in subsections 44(1) and 46(2), the Corporation is, for all purposes of this Act, an agent of Her

Majesty, and it may exercise its powers under this Act only as an agent of Her Majesty."

Property, 47 (3)

"Property acquired by the Corporation is the property of Her Majesty and title thereto may be vested in the name of Her Majesty or in the name of the Corporation"

The CBC is a Crown Corporation governed by the Board of Directors, which includes the President/CEO and the Minister of Canadian Heritage.

The President of the CBC is appointed by the Governor in Council, which is the Queen of England's representative in Canada.

Therefore, the only "independence" enjoyed by the CBC is vested in Her Majesty.

Decentralization

In 2008, Hubert Lacroix was personally appointed by then Prime Minister Stephen Harper, as the new president of the CBC.

Lacroix was a lawyer who specialized in mergers and acquisitions, and Harper had prior visions of dismantling the CBC, stem from his past ties to the anti-CBC Reform Party. It was a time of uncertainty for the corporation.

They began by cutting funding to certain productions and small city branches, then replaced most of the employees… including myself, who worked on the live studio broadcasts… with a digital system that could be run by a skeleton crew.

This added to even more centralized power as the regional stations were getting too small to operate, and therefore, distribution to these areas was transferred to larger centers.

In earlier times, every province had its own "master control" and everything that was aired in that province was broadcast directly from that particular province.

That freedom was eliminated by removing their ability to air their own content directly, and was replaced with centralized distribution. Today, all that is broadcast anywhere in Canada by the CBC, must first be sent to Toronto for the English side, and Montreal for the French side, which in turn will re-distribute the content back to their respective provinces.

Further cuts in staff came in the form of autonomous news reporting, where an individual is both the technician and the reporter. These new VJ's could now shoot, write and cut their stories without the need for an extra cameraman and editor.

In this new era of viruses and lockdowns, the CBC, and virtually all of mainstream media around the world have reached a new low in journalistic standards. The government and big Corp have attempted to monopolize the truth, and place themselves as the sole authority of content distributed to the public.

If alternative views exist on topics such as vaccinations, which can adversely affect your wellbeing and even cause your death, it is the media's duty and responsibility to offer to the public, an unbiased reportage of both sides of the story and let the public decide for themselves whether to subject themselves to this form of treatment.

Disclosing only one side of the story is mis-leading, and tantamount to treason.

If the media only offers one variable in an equation, how then can we realistically formulate a rational decision?

Shockingly, at the height of the "pandemic", it was disclosed to me that all relevant CBC employees received an email from the board of directors, advising them to adhere to a new directive regarding anti-mask, anti-lockdown and anti-vaccine protests, whereas they were to ignore the protestors and their views.

Never have I seen such media bias and outright censorship of information, outside of communist and totalitarian forms of rule. It is a blatant violation of journalistic codes and values, and assured we can be, that this directive was imposed directly from the political leaders of this country.

Chapter 2

POLITICS IN MEDIA

It is self-evident that governments should have no place in censoring media, or controlling its programming.

Politicians however, are easily coerced by corporate lobbyists and encouraged to pass legislation that helps to further the agendas of the global empire. The wealth and attention offered to them is hard to resist.

The act of lobbying itself is an important and legitimate process, allowing the public to be able to express their interests to government officials and influence their decisions regarding legislation and public policy. It is protected by the first amendment in the U.S. and by the lobbying Act in Canada, and many countries around the world have similar legislation.

However, "the problem is that lobbyists are routinely using money, favors, gifts, and lucrative job offers to do the convincing for them… put more simply, you can lobby, and you can donate money to a politician, but you should not be allowed to do both at the same time… it's like handing the referee fifty bucks before the game starts, and fifty thousand dollars right after the game…"[2]

Lobbying has become the norm in the political arena and their influence is so great that in reality, it is nothing less than legalized bribery. It is not uncommon for an elected official to commit political suicide by proposing outrageously unpopular acts of legislation. One might question their motives, until you consider the lucrative offers made to them by lobbyists, in return for their treachery.

In an interview on 60 Minutes,[3] former lobbyist Jack Abramoff admits to how easily they were able buy off congressmen and senators, especially with lucrative job offers, following their terms in office, acknowledging that their corrupt lobbying practices were indeed a form of bribery.

Investigations conducted for republicreport.org to uncover the salaries of lawmakers who did in fact become lobbyist after their political terms, reveals the substantial increase in their salaries.

"Our research effort uncovered the partial salaries of twelve lawmakers-turned-lobbyists. **Republic Report's investigation found that lawmakers increased their salary by 1452% on average** from the last year they were in office to the latest publicly available disclosure:"[4] – This article originally appeared on Republic Report – http://RepublicReport.org

In Canada, there is a five-year post-employment prohibition on lobbying imposed on former public office officials.

Incidentally, contrary to popular beliefs, politicians do not write laws, they pass laws. Since legislation is often brought forward by lobbyists, it is sometimes believed that they are responsible for writing our laws. Lobbyists however, are only hired as representatives for third party interests, and it would be more accurate to say that it is these corporations' lawyers that write the legislations presented to governments.

Writing laws is a very specialized process that requires a deep understanding of legalese, and knowledge of the entire legal system itself. Legalese is the language of law. Words are specifically defined to the laws in which they are written. It may seem like a law is written in English for example, yet the words used may not have the same meanings attributed to them in normal parlance.

To define certain words in one act of legislation, you sometimes have to refer to the definitions attributed to them in another act, and it can be very difficult to truly understand the implications concerning various acts, as you simply cannot find the true meaning behind the words. The entire law system therefore, has to be contained within a very organized structure, maintained by specialized individuals.

It is highly unlikely therefore, that any of our elected officials at all levels of government can even begin to understand the legislations they are voting on, further than the sales pitch given to them by the people trying to get these laws passed, or the lobbyists who represent their interests.

Eager politicians looking to advance their careers will see great opportunity in the offers made by lobbyists, and can be easily convinced to vote in favor of passing laws, in return for these lucrative offers.

Our elected representatives therefore become nothing more than salesmen working for the large corporate interests with deep pockets, and their job is to gain public support by convincing the population of the benefits of passing these laws, using the same sales pitch used on them by the lobbyists.

In a democracy, the leader of the political party in power will easily convince the members to support the legislation, while the opposition party will vote against the law, giving the illusion that there is a voice of opposition in parliament. A majority government will have no trouble passing laws, and in a minority government, you need only convince enough members of the opposition to make up the difference.

Our democracies are not the bastions of freedom venerated by today's society. We are led to believe we are free, yet it seems that the word "freedom" has lost its meaning.

True liberty comes from personal freedom. The right to live your own way, where the majority cannot force you to comply to rules that are not conducive to your moral standards and the freedom to express your true self.

Of course, we are all bound by natural law, yet beyond that are not obliged to live under the rules and laws of others who have concluded that we should serve the edicts provided by their society. It is for this reason that a republic is a preferred system, as it protects individual rights.

If popular science established one day that the use of coffee was a danger to family life, and would lobby the government to convince the majority of the population to support a new legislation banning the consumption of coffee in your own home, you would have then lost that right, hinged upon the popular support of a majority, who's values were effectively altered to support a law that is based on a science and philosophy that is underwritten by scientific data that is virtually unverified by the general population.

Ask yourself the following questions: How many scientific documents, journals or lab reports have I read in my lifetime? Do I truly understand how coffee beans are grown, harvested, processed, packaged and transported directly to my coffee mug every morning?

If I told you that the process of roasting coffee seeds involves 1500 chemical reactions, and that the plants are grown using countless chemicals found in pesticides and herbicides, and that the caffeine found in the beverage causes chronic conditions of all internal organs including the brain, upsets the cardiovascular system, increases blood pressure, causes fatigue, depression, neurasthenia, insomnia, arrhythmia and hypoglycemia… you could choose to either believe these statements and quit consuming coffee, research this information further and make your own decision, or ignore this message entirely… suppose however, that your choice could be influenced.

A government that is determined to ban the use of coffee would first introduce the new legislation for a first reading and proceed to promote the idea through a variety of means. They would send press releases to the media and air parliamentary debates. They would provide scientific documents to support their claims. They would engage scientists, laboratory technicians and doctors as representatives and supporters of this legislation. Media would produce content describing its harmful effects and expose the dangerous farming practices. They would seek out victims of this harmful product to personalize its damaging effects and to create an emotional reaction, subsequently demonizing any who support its use and opposes its ban. Famous personalities would be encouraged to belittle these antagonists, instigating a climate of mis-trust and fear towards the opposition, as the populace is slowly coerced towards choosing to side in favor of banning the product for fear of public condemnation.

The legislation would eventually be adopted through an apprehensive, yet generally submissive public, mis-directed by an involuntary free will.

We must remember that repetition is the key to persuasion. Media may air a piece regarding the dangers associated with drinking coffee, and it will be quickly forgotten by the general public. But it is the constant repetitious bombardment of information that will make the message sink in and become an issue.

Although we must recognize the benefits of an organized society, a truly informed populace would not require excessive legislation, as this power to enact laws would not be in the hands of corporate interests, but rather, controlled by the people for their benefit.

This type of freedom does not exist in ignorance and obedience, but in the strength of wisdom, truth, courage and responsibility. A callow and disconnected populace will inevitably fall prey to the wiles of the domineering, and become enslaved to their delusions.

In reality, we do not vote on whether or not to pass new legislation. In a democracy, we vote for our political party of choice, in the hope that they will actually be representing our ideologies and beliefs in parliament.

Political parties must recruit well-wishers from across the country to fund and manage their operation, and through the dispelling of empty words and promises, the master orators revered by the members quite easily manipulate the masses into fiercely defending their similar ideologies.

FLASHBACK...

I was the audio technician on a remote, covering a national party convention for a rather conservative group. We had a platform set up on the side of this large convention center banquet hall, and we decided to interview a political figure from a rival party which had been invited. We are live on the air nationally, and our stage lights suddenly go dark. I quickly discovered that an electrical cable had been unplugged from its socket. I plugged it back in and not 30 seconds later, the lights go off again. But this time we spotted party members unplugging the lights. We abruptly told them to leave and had to continue the interview amidst the entire crowd of hundreds of people chanting so loudly (some approaching the stage shouting profanities), that we were forced to stop the interview in progress.

I was dumbfounded at the fact that some of these people might become our leaders one day. They might have remembered after all, that they did invite this rival member to their convention.

(End of Flashback)

Politicians are very dependent on the media and they don't take kindly to anyone trying to impede on their career advancements. On the evening news, you will see short clips of our brave and fearless leaders. But behind the scenes they can be nasty.

I've seen a provincial Premier scream across a parking lot at a journalist simply because he believed a quote was used out of context and didn't make him look good. We can therefore understand the journalists' reluctance to truly expose anything of significance, and would rather confine themselves to mediocre "hit pieces".

A reporter walked into my editing booth to cut a story regarding leaders of several provinces in Canada, meeting to discuss trade relations. I was somewhat surprised as I already knew they were meeting to discuss the N.A.S.C.O. trade corridor initiative and was very well aware of the fact that it was not a popular subject amongst the parties involved, due to its controversial nature. I asked the journalist if this was indeed the basis of her story, but she had no knowledge of this subject and told me she was sent to cover what they had labeled the "Premier's Conference".

The North American Super Corridor Coalition (N.A.S.C.O.) is a non-profit organization with the goal of facilitating trade across Mexico to Canada through a multi-modal transportation system.

With the help of R.F.I.D. chips imbedded in product packaging, countries such as China can ship containers to Port Lazaro Cardenas in the southern tip of Mexico, load them onto trucks and transport them to the heart of the U.S. and Canada, bypassing border inspection, to central destinations such as Kansas City Smart Port and Center Port Canada in Winnipeg.

The trade corridor also extends north to the port of Churchill in northern Manitoba. The port was sold in 1997, to a U.S. company called Omnitrax for ten dollars. They also purchased a significant portion of the rail lines connecting Churchill to Winnipeg, in an effort to facilitate trade with Murmansk in Russia and Beijing, through northern Canadian shipping routes.

The port and railway were subsequently sold in 2018, to the **Arctic Gateway Group**, which is an arm of Canada's Gateways and Trade Corridors.

It's important to note that only a small fraction of the shipping containers entering our borders from foreign countries are actually physically inspected.

According to an article posted on the icontainer.com website, only 2% to 10% of shipping containers entering sea ports in most countries around the world are actually physically inspected.[5]

China presently owns and/or controls a multitude of North American and foreign ports and terminals in countries around the world.[6]

I grew up in the seventies and eighties at the tail end of the cold war, and was raised to believe that the communists were enemy number one. The news relentlessly expounded the threat of nuclear war and the evils of communism. To suggest in these times, that one day Russia and China would be able to send shipping containers directly to the heart of the U.S. and Canada un-inspected by customs, would have been akin to treason.

To put this in perspective...

The list of companies owned by the communist, People's Liberation Army (PLA) of China, is quite impressive. They are diversified in such industries as oil, technology, communication, steel, transportation, shipping, aircrafts, banking, automotive, agriculture, arts and entertainment, chemicals, energy, insurance, coal, pharmaceuticals, mining, cement and tobacco… to name a few.

China now also boasts the world's largest military force. According to the U.S. Defense Technical Information Center, China has 2.8 million active soldiers, 1 million reservists, approximately 15 million in the militia and a potential manpower of 200 million fit for service.[7]

The Chinese army would certainly be at an advantage, were they to plan an invasion.

Control of ports of entry allows shipping containers to be shipped directly to the heart of enemy territory unchecked, and allows for pre-positioning and distribution of weapons and artillery throughout the country.

Immigration policy enables strategic localization and pre-positioning of military personnel and integration of foreign personnel for gathering intelligence.

Control of ports and key transportation corridors allows for quick military mobilization.

An uninformed, ignorant and disarmed public, afraid of questioning the influx of foreigners due to fear of being persecuted as "racists", allows for easy integration.

Being a major supplier of food, industrial equipment, transportation devices, computers, cell phones and technology enables spying on a massive scale and allows for the sabotage of our transportation, food, and communications infrastructure.

Control of our legislature through lobbying, allows for laws to be passed to facilitate their plans.

Infiltration of our government allows for laws to be passed which regulate our media to ensure anonymity.

Shockingly, the U.S. and Canada are virtually completely dependent on rare earth minerals from China, which are crucial to the development of various commercial and military technologies.[8]

Is Russia and China strategically positioning themselves to facilitate a military coup against various countries? Time will tell. However, there are alternative methods of conquering a nation, as is clearly outlined by ex KGB defector, Yuri Bezmenov.

In 1970, Yuri Bezmenov, alias; Tomas David Shuman, a Russian translator and Novosti journalist who also worked as a KGB public relations agent hired to spread disinformation and propaganda to foreign countries, defected to Canada.

In an interview conducted in 1984 by G. Edward Griffin,[9] he outlined the Soviet brainwashing plan to morally destroy the U.S. through ideological subversion techniques.

This psychological warfare process is accomplished in four steps.

The first step is to undermine the moral values of the country by programming the people to see good as evil and vice versa, and make them act in ways that are inimical to their best interests to the point where they cannot recognize truth regardless of evidence to the contrary, and will condemn all those who challenge their ideologies or dissent against the system.

The second step is to create doubt and confusion within the populace, inciting internal conflict and hostility, and further destabilizing the country through economic hardships, as well as local and foreign threats to their way of life.

Through such threats, you can then create crisis points that will instill fear into the people and make them trusting and compliant to government mandates, subsequently giving away their rights and freedoms for a sense of perceived security.

Through mass media and public education, the new generations will be adapted to this demoralized and desensitized culture, and will even mock the axioms that make up a healthy society. They will be coerced into accepting moral depravity, indifference, self-indulgence, fascist adherence to Big Brother style doctrines and self-righteousness as the new normal, and will even come to despise themselves and their own country.

This method of conquering our country from within, has now become too obvious to ignore.

Our bought-out leaders are bound to the will of their masters, and can be easily seduced to deceive the public, as exemplified by our "Premier's Conference" ruse.

Naturally, politicians are never too eager to answer questions regarding controversial subjects, especially when meeting in secret with the private sector.

But, was this meeting actually kept a secret? Absolutely not.

The host province had a press release posted on their website stating the fact. It was also clearly stated on N.A.S.C.O.'s website, amongst numerous other websites of organizations involved with the project, as well as many alternative news sites describing the event.

How can it be possible that virtually no-one, including every single one of my co-workers in the newsroom, had any knowledge that this meeting was taking place? How can our elected officials have a meeting with the private sector, dealing with important international trade negotiations and border protection issues, and not be questioned by the media or confronted by the public in any way? More importantly, what makes them believe they have the right to meet away from the eyes of the public they are hired to serve?

There are absolutely no excuses that any government can make to justify keeping secrets from the public. You would not hire an accountant to take care of your finances and allow him/her to meet in secret with investors to discuss the future of your own estate. Yet that has become common practice with the governments of most countries today.

All that was needed to keep their meeting a "secret", was to first concoct another good reason to meet, and use it as a cover to hide the true agenda. The press release sent by the government noted the "Premier's Conference", and the journalists were sent out to report on this story, unaware of the actual purpose for the gathering.

This exemplifies the fact that news items are virtually un-researched, save the minimal requirements to actually write the story. The press release focused on the Premier's Conference, and accordingly, it was the story covered on the news.

In reality, anyone had access to all this information… yet very few will venture into the world beyond repetitive daily activities and social programming. We assume that our politicians are doing their job, and if anything was significant enough to warrant our attention, it would be disclosed to us through various media platforms.

Was the story factual?

The Journalist reported on a meeting of the Premiers, got the date, location, attendees and the reason for meeting correct… as they were in fact hosting a Premier's Conference. The media cannot be accused of lying, owing to the fact that they reported the truth, and have a group of high positioned government agents to support their claims.

The intended N.A.S.C.O meeting however, did also factually take place, but was not mentioned in any report.

Are the media reporting lies? Are they purposefully withholding facts?

There were no lies distributed throughout the media, and you cannot withhold facts that you don't even know exist. Therefore, the Government and their counterparts from the private sector were able to have a meeting, hidden in plain sight.

FLASHBACK…

I had to edit a voice over regarding the Prime Minister of Canada at the time, Stephen Harper, meeting with head scientists at the Center for Infectious Diseases in Winnipeg. I had two tapes of footage to work with. The first was thirty seconds long and the second was less than one minute in duration. The footage consisted of Harper sitting at a conference table with the ICID staff, which looked suspiciously uncomfortable. No one spoke of the reason for the meeting and no interviews were conducted. The media were allowed into the room for thirty seconds and then literally pushed out of the room by Harper's private security.

The meeting, the location and its participants were correctly identified by the reporter. However, no mention of the fact that we were not allowed to conduct interviews, know the true purpose of the meeting, or that we were treated as pests and thrown out of the office after thirty seconds.

We reported that they had a meeting and proceeded to guess as to its purpose.

(End of Flashback)

From a viewer's perspective, the meeting did take place, and the speculated report became factual information. Why? Because as a viewer, you need not prove your facts, therefore guesses can be discussed with family and friends as factual, and if questioned, you may point out that you heard it on the news.

It is somewhat akin to gossip and rumor mongering… and before long, as we mingle with co-workers and converse at the dinner table, most of us will be aware that the Prime Minister was meeting with the ICID staff, or that the province was hosting the "Premier's Conference" where they were to review trade and relations between provinces.

We were also informed by the news that it was good for the economy, as a few companies were going to make a few extra bucks that weekend.

There is something magical that happens to people when a sense of "profiting" from something is introduced into the equation. Suddenly, there is a bright side to which we can connect, and the purpose of the meeting in question becomes irrelevant.

Yet, if you remain observant, you will notice that we are never shown excerpts from the actual meetings. No one, including all of us in the media, are privy to what actually transpires behind the closed doors of bureaucracy.

They will meet in secret to discuss infectious disease situations because they don't want to create a "panic".

Budget meetings, trade conferences, international affairs meetings, national affairs meetings also merit discretion.

We can certainly agree that there are good reasons to merit prudence, yet we must consider the opaque nature of governmental transparency in this equation.

Our representatives are meeting with foreign dignitaries, lobbyists, international bankers, leaders of industry, scientists, and a long list of high rollers in the world of finance, and we have absolutely no idea what actually transpires during these talks.

It's important to consider the inherent dangers of government secrecy. You will notice that there are no examples in human history where such practices led to the prosperity of the working class.

The media does not question the system, it is written and directed by the system. Which is also quite apparent in our electoral process.

Elections

"Men said; 'We vote; we are offered the platform we want; we elect the men who stand on that platform, and we get absolutely nothing.' So they began to ask: 'What is the use of voting? We know that the machines of both parties are subsidized by the same persons, and therefore it is useless to turn in either direction.'"[36] *– Woodrow Wilson – 28th President of the United States*

It is common during elections to send a journalist and cameraman out on the street to meet with constituents and ask them for whom they are voting, and the reasons for their choice. I have edited countless of these which we call "streeters", and I can testify to its ability to reveal the extent to which the public is uninformed in matters of actuality.

When questioned on their choice of candidate, most will swiftly reply with surety, but when challenged on the reasons for their choice, they will hesitate and proclaim that the incumbent did a "good job" or that "we need a change".

Rarely have I heard anyone respond with an informed statement regarding their choice of candidates. In actual fact, if someone is truly informed, they already understand the futility of this endeavor and do not vote… or are too afraid to make a statement for fear of being ridiculed for their views.

Regardless, it is unlikely that their statement would ever make it on the news as we do not entertain "conspiracy theories".

Does your vote really matter?

In a sense it does, as the system does require your vote to legitimize the process. But when you consider the total lack of public understanding regarding governmental affairs… some even basing their decision on the merit that their preferred candidate was perceived as being "hot" … your vote becomes a commodity that can be easily purchased.

I conducted research on the last ten mayors to be elected in the city in which I lived at the time, and discovered that virtually every mayor elected was the one who had spent the most money. In the cases where they did not, the winning candidate had spent close to the same amount of money.

According to an article published on The Washington Post website by Wesley Lowery, nine times out of ten, the candidate who spent the most money won their election.[10]

Yes, elections can be bought…

In this day and age, the electoral process has become a circus of clowns. A childish game of finger pointing and name calling. There are no legitimate issues to be discussed and the media has no real questions to address. It is a popularity contest and the candidate with the deepest pockets wins. The media diligently reports on this side show attraction with serious intent and the public absorbs the carnival, unaware that the electoral process and political rhetoric is nothing more than a play being performed on a stage for an unsuspecting and trusting audience.

The game of politics however, can be difficult to grasp without first having an understanding of the game of law.

37

Chapter 3

THE GAME OF LAW

The rules we live by vary, depending on the country in which we live, and the system by which it is governed. It seems that throughout history, humankind has always struggled to maintain their freedom from oppressive governing bodies.

Most of us understand the fundamentals of natural law, and agree to its principles with regards to mutual respect in a functioning society, yet the subversion of our laws into legislations, bills, acts, executive orders etc., become the dictates of an oppressed society that only serve the ruling class who have in essence, confiscated our inherent dominion over our bodies and souls, by misleading us into giving up these responsibilities to a perceived higher authority.

In order to better understand the "game" of which I speak, imagine yourself being carried off and left stranded in an unfamiliar forest with one hundred other people, having no memory of who you are, where you came from, or anything from your life before the abduction.

Being faced with such circumstances, you will quickly realize the need for each other's help in order to survive. You will need clothing, food, shelter etc. As you build your homes and community, the need for roads become evident. Some are not capable of defending themselves and require protection from the few who would take advantage of the weak and elderly. Surely, there should be a system in place to manage the communal resources and infrastructure, as well as to provide support and protection to the community, in a framework of societal limits and consequences.

However, if we are all inherently created equal, how can anyone be the judge of another? How are the rules of this society to be enforced? How can anyone have the right to assault and incarcerate another against their will?

The solution is to create a game where one may become a member, and as a member, must abide by its laws, and in return, reap the benefits of an organized society… i.e., government, money, police, fire trucks, maintained roads, social assistance etc.

We shall call this game the "Law Society", and your pawn in the game is a corporation created in your name at birth.

In our common use of the English language, we may define the word "person" as a flesh and blood human being, but in law, a "person" is defined as a "corporation".

Another benefit of joining this society is that you would also own a share in the corporation invented in the name of the country in which you live, and profit from the immense wealth of the country.

If you had no need for such a system, or did not agree with its laws, you were still left with the option to renounce your membership to the society. However, as was common practice in old kingdoms, such a person would be labelled an "outlaw", unprotected by the law, to be hunted down and killed.

It was a plot of intimidation to ensure that every person remain bound to the laws of the society.

This law system is based on Maritime law, or Admiralty law, and your name actually represents a ship.

When a ship comes to its berth… or a mother gives birth… a berth/birth certificate signed by the dock/doctor must be produced.

A ship delivers products through a water canal, as a mother delivers through water and a birth canal.

Money represents water. it is liquidity, cash flow…

Banks control the flow of money, or currency, such as river banks control the flow of water, or current of the sea. If the water is frozen, it is not allowed to flow, like frozen assets impede the flow of money.

As long as you understand the game and remain Captain of your Ship… i.e., a Sovereign human being in control of your Corporation, you may reap the benefits of this Law Society. However, if you fail to maintain your responsibilities, or are incapable of doing so, your Corporation may be hijacked and used against your best interests.

When parents register their newborn baby by signing a birth certificate, they are in fact giving away ownership of their child to a foreign entity… aka the CROWN… and a Corporation/LEGAL FICTION is created in the child's given name.

The birth certificate then becomes a financial instrument, a bond that can be sold and traded on the market, and you will be treated as a product without rights, including ownership rights to your own flesh.

As a PERSON with no rights, you are considered incompetent, and unable to take care of yourself or legally stand before a judge, and therefore, an Estate Trust is created for your benefit, and the management of your Estate… including your physical body… is put in the care of a capable and competent authority.

A series of what are called Cestui Que Vie Trusts are created to seize control of your Estate, and strip you of all individual rights and freedoms… including the rights to your own human body… and will also claim ownership of the title to your soul. Without title to your soul, you are nothing more than a product/cargo/stock, a ship that is lost or abandoned at sea, which can then be salvaged according to the rules of Maritime Law.

You then become chattel… a slave to the Vatican Roman Cult which controls the system.

In 1302, a Papal Bull called the Unum Sanctum was signed by Pope Boniface, claiming in trust, the entire world and everything upon it, including all human souls.

Our lives, our work, our children, our possessions, our land, our bodies, our bank accounts and our souls are registered property owned by the Vatican.

How were they able to accomplish such a bold and cunning deception?

If the system was created to be of benefit to humanity, how did we end up living under the "rule" of another, as nothing more than chattel slaves?

While it is true that one may only gain power over another sovereign through force or consent, there is another "power" which holds dominion over all men/women. No one could deny the power of "God".

Therefore, if one could convince the populace that they were given the "divine right" to rule and judge... one could become kings and queens or religious leaders with immense power and influence.

If you form an organization, amass immense wealth through corruption, coercion, sabotage, murder and the control of money, construct impressive buildings and statues from where you operate, and have the members of your association idolize and worship the leader of this organization in public and private ceremony's, venerated as ruler "by divine right", you could surely make enough of an impression amongst the commoners to deceive them into believing that your leader is a divine messenger of "God".

Or at the very least, be so feared by the population as to not be challenged.

Have you ever wondered why politicians will pass laws that are detrimental to our way of life?

Have you ever wondered why protesting does not work?

Have you ever wondered why politicians don't seem to listen to the people by whom they are employed?

After all, they are but our employees, are they not?

The United States, Canada, and virtually every country in the world, are in fact corporations. They are Crown colonies that are owned by the Jesuit/Vatican global empire and controlled by the three City States. Our elected officials work for the corporation, not the people.

The three City States are; the City State of London (the financial arm), Washington D.C., or the District of Columbia (the military arm), and the Holy See, or Vatican City State (the religious arm). These are private corporations operating independently from the countries in which they are located, and have their own laws, police, banks, flags etc.

Canada operates under a constitutional monarchy, and all bills and acts of legislation must receive Royal Assent before being passed into law. In other words, the Crown must approve all of its laws, which is done through the Governor General, which is a representative of the Queen, which is the lifetime hereditary head of state of Great Britain and her colonies. Provincial legislation receives Royal Assent through their respective Lieutenant Governors, which are also representatives of the Crown, appointed by the Governor General of Canada.

It is not by mere coincidence that the Queen of England is known to most as a simple figurehead with no real power.

This grave mis-representation was purposefully enacted to camouflage the sweeping powers and influence retained by this group of individuals we refer to as "Royalty", and it is through the game of law that they have secured their positions as rulers.

For what other purpose would governmental institutions and property be referred to as Crown Corporations or Crown land, and for what other reason would we need the Queen's permission to pass any law, were it not for the Crown Corporation's claims on such chattels?

The public is largely unaware of the true power that the Queen possesses, as she protects herself from political conflicts by delegating her powers, which include:

- The power to refuse legislation passed by parliament

- The power to dissolve parliament and call new elections

- The power to declare war without parliamentary approval

- The power to choose or dismiss the prime ministers

- The power to enact laws

- The power to declare a state of emergency

And more…

We have all heard the Queen refer to us as her "subjects".

As a "subject", you owe your allegiance to another, such as a sovereign.

A Sovereign has supreme power and authority over themselves, such as a Queen or a King, meaning that they have lawful control and authority over their LEGAL FICTION, as well as their own body and flesh, and are not governed by an outside authority.

Laws, legislation, regulations and executive orders only apply to the corporations in the game.

Does humanity really need rulers? Do we need to be governed? It does seem like a great number of people have a natural propensity to follow the leader. Personalities determine the pecking order. Some, possessing certain combinations of traits, are pre-dispositioned to play the part of our leaders.

Given the condition of our present social system, structured in a manner in which to filter in the right candidates for the job, we are left with leaders who are bought and paid for by the ruling class with promises of fame and fortune.

Truth is… they can deliver.

When you own and control virtually everything, your influence is unmatched.

Therefore, the job attracts "leaders" who care more about money and personal gain, rather than the people they are entrusted to serve.

A truly informed and enlightened society would have no real need for leadership. Only public servants to manage the State.

True liberty however demands personal responsibility and commitment to the preservation of these rights, and a media that is accountable to the people.

If you are unaware that a problem exists, a solution cannot be formulated. The right answers are therefore inexorably linked to your ability to ask the right questions.

But how does one formulate a right question? How do you know that the knowledge you have accumulated throughout your lifetime is actually true? You might be of the opinion that what you believe is true, stems from the fact that it is "common knowledge". If everyone believes something to be true, then it must be true… right?

If I tell you that weather modification is possible and is actually being used today, you might not believe me. Yet this information is factual, and not hidden… as we can see from this treaty signed in 1975, by Canada and the United States.

"The government of Canada and the Government of the United States of America,

Aware, because of their geographic proximity, that the effects of weather modification activities carried out by either Party of its nationals may affect the territory of the other;

Noting the diversity of weather modification activities in both Canada and the United States by private parties, by State and Provincial authorities, and by the Federal Governments;"[11] – *Treaty - E103819*

I was approached by a co-worker several years after I had left the CBC, and he mentioned a few interactions he had with other co-workers who had come to notice the now too obvious to ignore fascist takeover of our country, admitting that my daily dose of facts were indeed correct, and wondered how I was able to predict future events.

Yet I've always maintained that these facts are not hidden, and there is no prediction involved. It is only the stated endgame of their plans. No one ever predicts the future; they are only privy to the plan. Although some information might be more of a challenge to find, and some even inaccessible, there is enough available to deduce the obvious.

Why would a person not believe something that is true? Is it because they didn't hear it on the evening news? Or perhaps it is because of the most effective brainwashing scheme ever created… the most destructive two words ever combined… the words "conspiracy theory".

Don't tell me, I don't want to know…

Here we must introduce one of the greatest and most powerful of human motivators… hard wired into every mind… the fear of being ridiculed. No one wants to look like a fool, especially not labeled as a tin foil hat wearing conspiracy theorist. A survival instinct perhaps? Whatever the case, it has proven to be one of the most persuasive deterrents to an informed society ever devised.

Any information that resembles the label "conspiracy theory" will automatically provoke sensations of fear and mistrust, and be ignored and avoided to the point where most people will not dare instigate such conversations, for fear of rejection or ridicule.

Journalists fear this label more than any other. They will not touch upon any subject stamped with this distinction, as they risk permanent ostracization from the field of journalism.

In other words, the people we entrust to keep us informed of important current events, will not touch upon any information, or write any story regarding any subject with the label "conspiracy theory", regardless of its importance to our well-being. It is journalistic suicide.

This same apprehension extends to the majority of employees in all departments in the field of media, and therefore, any alternative information having the hope of reaching the airwaves is filtered through employees that base their decisions regarding the content that is to be made public, through fear.

Fear of being ridiculed by their peers or the public, fear of losing their job, fear of not fitting in at their workplace or in society in general, fear of ostracization from their friends and family, fear of the law and of the government, fear of facing the possibility that the conspiracy theories might be true, fear of the wellbeing of their families, and a host of other fears that are used against the person to assure obedience to the dictates of accepted societal norms.

The news media personnel is therefore left to operate within the walls of policy and mediocracy, and it is the fate that one must endure to work in the industry.

I remember a past incident where Russia attacked Georgia. I read otherwise and told the reporter covering the story that it was Georgia that had instigated the conflict. He refuted my claims. Yet nearly a year later, this same journalist walks into my editing suite with a look of excitement on his face and tells me I was right. Evidently, the journalistic world had finally decided to accept this fact. I knew the same day that it happened.

Why is it that a bottom of the pyramid technician sitting in his editing suite can easily spend fifteen minutes on the internet on a few somewhat reliable sites, and find more accurate information about worldly events than what is presented by the mainstream news outlets we rely on for our information?

I recall an occasion where a journalist walked into my editing suite bouncing with excitement at the big headline story that he had just uncovered… turns out that he had noticed that the windows at the legislative building were not sealed properly, which meant they were not energy efficient, which in the climate of energy efficiency so promoted by the government at the time, seemed important enough to this journalist to merit a "breaking news" status. I chose to withhold my opinion, as he was so proud of his discovery that I didn't want to hurt his feelings by pointing out the frivolous nature of his story.

I remember overhearing the editor in chief conversing with a colleague in the cafeteria one particular afternoon, complaining that it was a tranquil day in the newsroom because he was having difficulty striking up any newsworthy subjects to cover. I could have easily suggested a dozen topics off the top of my head that deserved the headline that day.

Naturally, these employees were limited by the policies of the organization when referring to the lack of newsworthy material, but additionally, were delineated by their total ignorance to any substance that exceeds the boundaries of these policies.

Knowledge is Power

Although the general truth is exposed for all to see, there are certain details surrounding any conspiracy that are carefully hidden and difficult to access.

If you pick an important subject and learn everything you possibly can about this subject… i.e., read profusely, interview people, ask questions, send emails, research the sources of information, make your friends and family question your sanity, get in trouble at work… it can, and most certainly will, inevitably lead to the same outcome… a dead end.

If you manage to dig far enough into a subject and uncover everything you possibly can with the resources at hand… if you learn proper definitions and use the right words to formulate the right questions, you will meet your fate at the altar of the zone of silence. Your questions will no longer be answered and your journey will come to a bitter end. Only those with the proper status and credentials may enter… and that is a long and dirty road of politics and money. Those of us at the base of the pyramid are not privy to such information.

We must however, ask the question; why should any information be withheld from anyone? Who are these guardians of knowledge? What power has bestowed upon them the right to edit what we can and cannot know? How can one be more worthy of knowledge than another?

The Vatican openly flaunts their gigantic library of ancient texts. Why do we not have access to this priceless information? Is it "their" texts? I can certainly understand the need to preserve such manuscripts. Why not then transcribe or photograph as many as possible and make them available to the general public on the internet? It is not within anyone's right to dictate who gets to have access to this wealth of information. Control of information is the definition of tyranny.

The excuses made by the government to justify withholding information from the public, are the same used in every dictatorship… the safety and security of the people and its country.

But when secrecy becomes the norm and the people are left ignorant, tyranny is always the end game. There are no records in history to refute this claim.

If knowledge is power, then how can lack of knowledge bring safety and security?

Are we in the media, guilty of hiding knowledge? It would be more accurate to say that we in the media are not privy to any information that would be worthy of hiding.

Anything controversial to the norms established by society is completely ignored. Offending a group or an individual is something that is avoided at all cost.

FLASHBACK…

We were in the middle of a provincial election and one of the local candidates managed to get an email list of the employees at the station and were relentlessly sending daily emails. Annoyed by their promotional rhetoric, I decided to offer a polite reply.

I told them that we were interested in covering a certain subject… which I knew they would not want to touch upon… and tried to arrange a time where we could send a cameraman and journalist over for an interview.

What happened next is a prime example of how media is controlled. The next day, I was called in for a board meeting.

Anything that threatens our policies and political correctness is met with immediate inquiry and disciplinary action. You must face the board… let me paint the picture…

You walk into a room centered by a large table surrounded by comfortable office chairs, upon which sits two union reps, your supervisor, his supervisor, human resources, and the producer.

They proceeded to tell me that they had received a call from a concerned delegate regarding a certain email that I had sent. They informed me that in order to ensure that this would not happen again, I would be suspended from work until such a time until the elections were completed.

I must admit that I was somewhat shocked at this swift and harsh action. I was testing the grounds to see if the subject in question would hit a nerve and it surely did. When it comes to winning elections, they do not take such chances.

I was attempting to explain to the board the reasons why I believed we should cover the story… as my union rep was kicking me under the table to stay quiet… but the board's only interest was protecting the political party from unwanted publicity, and protecting themselves from any controversy. The whole thing was blamed on improper usage of company property and no one would ever know how the party that won the election that year was deliberately hiding information from the public, and were able to easily manipulate the public broadcaster into helping them achieve this deception.

(End of Flashback)

But as far as the management staff were concerned, they were just doing their job and did not understand the significance of their actions.

Why is it that this management staff believed that "their job" was to protect the political establishment? Why did they not instead take into consideration the fact that the party in question was trying to hide information from the public? Why would the media try to protect themselves from controversy? Isn't it their job to expose such political secretiveness?

More importantly, why did this political organization require media censorship of such material? Alike the media, are they not accountable to the public they serve?

We ought to examine the pyramidal structure of these institutions to solve this dilemma.

I, as a bottom of the pyramid wage earner, am accountable to my supervisor, which is obliged to impose the regulations prescribed to his/her position. Adherence to the policies governing the corporation is ensured by local management, which are accountable to head office administration, which are liable to the vice-president, which answers to the president/CEO, which is a member of the board of directors and is appointed by the Governor in Council, which is a representative of the Crown.

Provincial governments, as we already know, answer to their respective Lieutenant Governors, which are representatives of the Crown, appointed by the Governor General.

We can now easily see that the policies governing the media, as well as the political arena, both stem from the Crown, and through these written policies, they were able to effortlessly manipulate the CBC employees and the politicians involved into believing that their job was to suppress the information I had brought to light, and therefore, issue my temporary suspension.

The higher management staff and the party leaders are easily convinced to strictly apply the policies of the Corporation down the chain of command. They are made to feel a sense of importance and high social status, as they are invited to attend high level corporate meetings and become members of various clubs where they live a more lavish life and have access to a wealthier crowd of people that can help them skyrocket their career.

Questioning the corporate policies, or accommodating the rants of a dis-obedient employee is not considered, and may even be viewed as a threat to their personal success. Climbing the corporate ladder and becoming a member of even more exclusive clubs is paramount.

I was reading through a list of Bilderberg Group attendees invited at the 2010 conference, and noticed something interesting. For those of you who are not familiar, the Bilderberg Group is a secretive, exclusive club comprised of super rich elitists such as David Rockefeller and other globalists such as Henry Kissinger, Queen Beatrix, Bill Gates any many more, which host an annual conference in high class hotels around the world. Invited participants include heads of state and leaders in the fields of finance, industry, academia and… you guessed it… the media.

They are often referred to as the "president makers".

I noticed that the beloved host of our national news program, Peter Mansbridge, was on the list of 2010 attendees. So, I decided to write him an email and inquire as to how the meeting had transpired, and added that I was looking forward to his report on the national program.

Suffice it to say that he did not reply to my email… and certainly did not report it on the news.

In other words, CBC's most prominent figure, featured on our daily national news program, attended a secret meeting with people who essentially rule the media, financial, educational, political, and industrial sectors of the world, and would not discuss his involvement in this secretive club with CBC staff or the public who pays his salary.

Is there truly a conspiracy to rule the world by an international organization? Of course, and here are some of the highlights of the methods used to accomplish this goal.

1st – **Control the food supply**. (How many of us grow our own food these days)

2nd – **Control the money system**. (How many of us actually understand how money is created)

3rd – **Control knowledge**. (Knowing all the names of every hockey player in the NHL is not a threat to the establishment)

4th – **Control the political arena**. (Keep us busy complaining about bad road conditions and taxes)

5th – **Control the media**. (Keep everyone distracted with things that are not a threat to the goal of ruling the world)

If you create a corporate structure, built of employees with varying levels of accountability and knowledge, and place yourself at the top of this pyramidal construct, you need only control the corporations that supply the world with the essentials of life, and you can dictate policy down the chain of command from the CEOs to the low paid laborers with ease, and virtually everyone on the lower levels of this pyramid would be completely unaware of the sinister plot behind the policies.

What did our famous host learn at this Bilderberg conference? We'll never know. Truthfully, he is just another pawn being used to send a message through the chain of command. They certainly know how to make an impression. You are driven to a secret meeting at a posh hotel and greeted like a dignitary, as you proceed to mingle and make connections with the most powerful people in the world.

If you play the game, you will be rich and famous and live a life of luxury… if you decide to spill the beans on their diabolical plans, they will retaliate by sending "their people" to your home to perform the most atrocious of acts towards you and your family as you watch in horror. Not a hard decision for most.

By coincidence, the Bilderberg Group decided to meet in my native country of Canada one particular year. I decided that I was going to drive there and see this for myself. I recruited my friend and neighbor… young man, late twenties, paranoid, loved smoking weed, long dark curly hair that would stick out from beneath this toque that he wore religiously and looked like it was ready to shoot off his head at any moment… and the next morning we hopped in my caravan and drove 26 hours to Ottawa where the meeting was being held. We rented a hotel room that night and drove to the site in the morning.

A small group of people were gathered on the street facing the hotel. The entire compound was off limits, surrounded by security guards and patrolled by local law enforcement. But the real security came in the form of CIA, CSIS, MI5, Mossad and any other "intelligence" agency that was deemed necessary. We were told that if we decided to unexpectedly start running towards the building, we would be fired upon.

They were very serious about their security… patrols with guard dogs, snipers, total perimeter lockdown with a single guarded access where we could witness an endless stream of black limousines driving in and out of the compound with our fearless leaders hiding their faces behind darkened windows.

Did I mention that my neighbor is paranoid? It was at about this point when I realized that my faithful companion had no idea what he was getting into when he embarked on this journey. He was starting to turn pale and was incessantly prancing back and forth, looking completely uncomfortable in his skin, then turns to me and says, "I gotta get outta hear man… like right now!". Fully aware that he was starting to look a little suspicious… even raising the eyebrows of the protestors… I gave him the keys to the van and told him to meet me here at the end of the day.

I spent the rest of the afternoon hanging out in front of the building, mingling with prominent figures from around the world and ended up in a documentary produced by one of the most famous characters in the world of independent media.

We were gathered in this place, on this cold and rainy day, fists in the air, taking photographs, shooting video, observing this surreal environment, feeling more like we were on the scene of a Hollywood action movie rather than in our own reality.

We were here to send a message to the people that barricade themselves from the eyes of the world in secret meetings and believe that they have the right to control our lives… that message was clear… "Don't worry, only a handful of people showed up at the protest, you have managed to quell opposition to your plans for world domination to the point where no one really cares. Nice job… keep up the good work".

Interesting group of people however, no real incidents to report… although one guy was fairly exited that he had found a cap of oil in the grass around the protest site.

It was late afternoon when I finally heard back from my partner gone missing in action. He had decided to go spend the afternoon in a local pub and was now completely inebriated, determined that he was going to come back and storm directly through the compound in the van and make it to the front doors of the hotel.

I managed to convince him that it was not such a good idea and decided that now, might be a good time for me to leave the area. So, we met at a nearby parking lot and we got back in the van and drove 26 hours home.

Sobering up a bit on the drive home, he later told me that he had decided not to heed my warnings regarding making sure he didn't bring any contraband with him at the protest site. We found a good hiding spot in the van before we left and I was assured that all of it was in there. However, unbeknownst to me, he had decided to make an exception and pocket one particular item… his cap of oil… which he had apparently thrown in the grass back at the protest site, in fear of being caught.

Protests

Although revered as an inalienable human right necessary for the preservation of liberty, peaceful protesting is relatively useless. By lawful definition, when you protest to someone, you are actually acknowledging their power to deny your demands.

To put it in perspective, what possible threat to the establishment can a group of individuals chanting songs and picketing at the doorsteps of government buildings pose, to an organization that is defended by well-armed riot police and private security forces equipped with the latest in policy enforcement technology… and backed by a well-armed military?

Having attended a variety of peaceful protests, I can attest to the fact that they are brimming with passionate, loving, intelligent and interesting individuals. In general, it is a highly uplifting and positive experience.

How ironic is it, that a community of peaceful demonstrators and activists, united in the name of peace and love, are habitually met with armed law enforcement actively scanning license plates and creating databases of the protestors, scouring the flock for opportunities to flaunt their "power", and creating a general sense of un-easiness amongst the demonstrators.

Doubly ironic is that the people assigned with the important task of preserving the peace, suddenly become the aggressors, and will threaten, arrest, beat, taser, tear gas and use any means at their disposal to preserve that peace. And if there is no "peace" to be found, they will send in members of their own personnel to incite some "peace".

However, the observant protestors are not so easily fooled, and the deceitful provocateurs are occasionally exposed and confronted.

During the Security and Prosperity Partnership (SPP) meeting held in August of 2007 at the Chateau Montebello in Quebec, an incident occurred where a couple of thugs wearing handkerchiefs on their faces began inciting violence amongst the protestors, trying to persuade them to throw rocks at the windows of a nearby building.

Not falling for the bait, the demonstrators pointed them out as instigators and began gathering around the thugs to confront them.

They were now cornered against a building with the protestors at their front and the police line to their side.

One of the thugs walked over to the line and quietly spoke to one of the riot cops. Suddenly, the two men who were inciting violence threw themselves into the police line where they were brought down, handcuffed, and quickly taken away.

As they were pinned down, the demonstrators noticed that the thugs were wearing the exact same boots worn by the police who made the arrests.

The whole scene was recorded by several cameras and could not be ignored.

A colleague of mine covering the event, addressed the issue live on our national network.

Quebec police were forced to admit at a press conference that they had indeed deployed undercover officers into the crowd to incite violence. We were told that these agents were sent in as measures to weed out any violent protestors.

In other words, the agents were sent in to make sure that no violence occurred, by inciting violence.

Apparently sufficient as an excuse, the media moved on and never spoke of it again in future newscasts.

The public only needed to be convinced by a somewhat rational explanation, and the incident was quickly forgotten.

The peaceful protest was established for the following purposes:

1- Deceive the general public into believing they have a voice
2- Manipulate public opinion
3- Generate fear
4- Generate apathy towards important subjects
5- Generate disdain towards those who oppose government mandates
6- To justify the use of force against the people, and to acclimatize the general public to the rightness and necessity of its usage

In essence, it is a script for the press, as these strategies are all dependent on media support.

You must attend a demonstration, then subsequently watch the news coverage of the event, in order to appreciate the spin and distorted views employed by the media to paint a picture which in no way resembles the event in question.

FLASHBACK…

I was present at a freedom rally in a small city, accompanied by approximately two hundred demonstrators from all walks of life and age groups. Knowledgeable speakers conveyed messages of peace, love, freedom and truth. All who attended were peaceful and respectful of each other in an atmosphere of friendship and unity.

The rally ended with a long convoy of decorated vehicles driving through the city, honking horns and waving at supporters, respecting all driving regulations.

Noticing the media presence at the rally, I remember thinking to myself that the public will now be able to see the peaceful nature of these rallies and hear the important messages being conveyed.

However, the news coverage of the event on the following day fell nothing short of disgraceful.

The protestors were demonized as dis-respectful law breakers that should be fined and arrested for having the audacity to speak their minds.

Not one interview was conducted, not one voice heard, and not a single view-point from any of the demonstrators was shared with their audience.

Alternatively, law enforcement and local politicians were given a voice and portrayed as heroes and great leaders who were dismayed at the apparently inconsiderate protestors who dared to defy their authority.

The deified police performed their sworn duty to protect and serve, and kept the fearful public safe and secure from this menace to society.

The fact is however, that it was quite comical to witness the police frantically racing back and forth trying to get ahead of the convoy and maintain control of a situation which did not merit such actions. Their unwarranted behavior was analogous to having 5 units dispatched to a daycare center to go break up a fight between six-year old's.

A responsible media would have interviewed demonstrators, produced clips of the speakers, and delivered an unbiased reportage of the event.

(End of Flashback)

The ease with which the government can manipulate a scenario through the media was exemplified at the trucker's freedom convoy.

Over a million people were peacefully gathered at the parliament building in Ottawa, dancing, singing, giving away food to the homeless and stimulating their local economy. During the rally, crime dropped considerably… and some local elderly persons were pleased at the fact that they could actually go for walks around their neighborhood in safety.

The whole demonstration was completely vilified by the Prime Minister and the media, repeatedly referring to this one particular person that was seen garnishing a flag adorned with a swastika. This one agent provocateur… buried amongst a million protestors… was used to characterize the entire group of demonstrators, as racists and bigots.

Logically speaking, any intelligent human being would question using only one millionth of a group to represent the whole. Yet none of our elected officials, on either side of the political arena, chose to question this utter nonsense… which of course entirely exposes the game and the true allegiance held by these "public servants".

Reversely, protestors may also serve another important purpose. Unpopular legislation and controversial subjects can alarm citizens to the point where they believe action should be taken against such matters.

Organizations are specifically developed for the purpose of recruiting well-wishers who are courageous and motivated enough to do something in honor of their cause, and are subsequently used as pawns for these schemes of distraction and manipulation.

These tactics are ingeniously designed to make the listener believe that there is always someone "out there" taking action and raising concerns regarding any important or controversial subject, reassuring the viewer that no effort is required on their part, as someone else has already taken action.

This type of apathy has infected a large portion of the population, and through a multitude of social programming schemes, we are led to believe that there is always a super hero, a savior or a person of great strength and intelligence that will always be there to save the day. It is a con to make us believe that we do not have to take responsibility for certain aspects of our lives.

In this manner, personal rights and freedoms can easily be eroded, as the inattentive citizenry remain unconcerned, and are further coerced into becoming spies for the establishment.

Spies 'R' Us

We are taught from an early age to be government informants… see something, say something, don't think for yourself, call 911, tell the teacher, spy on your neighbors, don't assume responsibility, let someone else take care of things for you.

Teaching our children this kind of ideology can only lead to creating a society where no one is safe. Our neighbors, co-workers, friends and even family members become spies for the establishment.

Dictators have always relied on this ploy to quell dissent and weed out those who oppose their method of governing.

You need only establish a fear-based system of rules and regulations, justify it with good intentions, and society will police itself. Anyone who steps out of line with societal acceptance and political correctness is immediately feared, singled out, ratted on, and punished by the general public, and even by friends and family.

It is a tactic that has been repeatedly used throughout history, and is still quite relevant today.

Who then can we trust?

As you intensely study the system and become increasingly aware of its immense influence on our lives, you feel a need to share this information.

As I began to share some of these revelations with my co-workers, I quickly realized that if I were to make an impression, I would be obliged to have my facts in order.

I worked in an environment of educated and respected journalists and producers. One did not just make fantastic claims and expect to be taken seriously.

I was now determined to dive down the rabbit hole of information and dig as far as I could to learn every aspect of any subject I was studying, therefore, being armed with undeniable facts, they would have no choice but to consider my requests to add real content to the program.

Being somewhat naive, I actually believed that the reason no one took action was because they just didn't know… I ignorantly thought that if I could present them with factual information regarding important subjects, they would have no choice but to write a story and put it on air. What happened instead, was shocking.

Frustrated by the lack of interest in my bid to address real news on our show, I made no effort to give up my resolve and proceeded to let my opinion known wherever I felt it was needed. No one was spared from my daily dose of facts.

It was at this point where ridicule turned to fear.

Following the attacks of 9/11, the climate around terrorism became considerably elevated and everyone had suddenly become suspect. We were encouraged to report anything suspicious. Anyone could be a terrorist... watch your friends and neighbors.

One particular day, I was having one of my regular conversations with a colleague of mine with whom I had worked closely with for over fifteen years. Although he didn't share my views, he was accustomed to hearing my rants on freedom and change. That day, amidst all this terrorist paranoia he declares "maybe you're a terrorist... I don't know".

I was completely shocked! How could this person who had known me for so long, seriously proclaim such a statement? I was a peace-loving man... attended peace rallies, concerned with the fact that my country is being systematically destroyed and the company for which I worked was helping them to achieve this goal. I was standing up for what is right. Now being shunned as a possible "terrorist" conspirator?

It was at that moment that I became cognizant of the efficacy of the mind control techniques being utilized to manipulate the public into a heightened state of fear and suspicion.

In another instance, I was called in for another board meeting to discuss the fact that I had been sending emails to certain co-workers regarding important subjects. I told them that I wouldn't go to the meeting unless they showed me evidence of their claims. They produced photo-copies of emails that I was sending to a co-worker… a long-time work friend… addressed to the supervising staff with the heading… "here is another email from…" … me.

Fearful of being condemned by his peers, or being associated in any way with this "crazy guy", he was forwarding my emails to our supervisors.

But the real shocker came in the form of a committee, formed by a group of co-workers who were afraid… and annoyed… by my controversial opinions. They appointed a representative to whom they could deliver their complaints about me, so that it may be presented to the supervising staff for immediate action against my unacceptable insubordination.

In other words, a group of co-workers organized a committee, as a means to more efficiently tattletale on me.

I have no doubt that they would turn in their mother if she showed signs of "terrorist" activity… such as verbally challenging the policies of our government… which happens to be a crime now in our country.

Any who dare question the established doctrines will be silenced, censored, threatened, and even eliminated if necessary.

It is important to recognize those who've had the courage to expose corruption in the face of personal harm, and those throughout history who have sacrificed so much for the preservation of liberty. The true heroes were not the ones who signed the documents, but the common people who had the foresight to recognize the importance of taking action, and risked everything to ensure that future generations could inherit this freedom.

They might have re-considered their actions had they known that their sacrifices would be squandered away for sex, drugs, and rock 'n' roll.

The responsibilities necessary to preserve liberty have been subverted to suit a nefarious agenda, and the crucial elements essential to those ends are lost in a warped sense of patriotism, initiate at a young age though our public school system.

Chapter 4

PUBLIC SCHOOLS, THE GOOD CITIZEN

Our public school systems take advantage of the most crucial time in a child's development to imbue into their minds an ideological framework designed to effectively indoctrinate them into a counterfeit reality.

The experiences and knowledge gained from birth through adolescence will essentially define the individual for life, and the system is meant to hijack this crucial growth period in a person's life to effectively incarcerate the mind in an ideological prison.

It is designed to strip the children of their love of learning, and force them to work in a competitive landscape which honors good behavior with petty rewards and grading systems.

Public schools deprive you of your individuality, creativity, and independence of thought. You are taught to conform to rules, schedules, methodologies, and a standardized vision of the reality in which we exist.

It destroys your curiosity to the point where you will cease to ask questions, and fear those who dare challenge the system, creating a submissive society of good citizens who follow the rules and are afraid of any form of dissent.

The process is well documented by many individuals, politicians, journalists, educators, and authors such as John C. Holt, Henry Louis Mencken, Russel Ackoff, Charlotte Iserbyt, and many more.

Naturally, we cannot deny the importance of reading, writing, mathematics, science, history etc... however, we must question the authenticity of the material presented, and the methods utilized to teach these various subjects.

Have you ever wondered who writes the textbooks taught in our public schools?

I have researched this subject and was never able to accurately answer this question.

According to Charlotte Iserbyt, senior policy advisor in the U.S. Department of Education under President Ronald Reagan, whistle blower and author of the book "The Deliberate Dumbing Down of America", our school curriculum is based on a communist system.

Since all dictatorships are reliant on an apprehensive public which polices itself, we are indoctrinated into being fearful and suspicious of everyone, and having been trained from a young age to tell on others, it ensures continued acquiescence to this philosophy into adulthood, in a system replete with methods to encourage the same behavior.

Teaching children to surrender their power to "authoritative figures" will engender a lifelong trusting relationship with those whom they were made to believe have the "authority" to act in their stead, ensuring unwavering obedience to these perceived "authorities".

Once we graduate, we are thrown to the wolves to scratch a living, and are virtually ignorant to the way the system actually functions. We find a job, or skip from one to the next, barely making ends meet, and remain confined by the limits imposed upon us by our infamous schooling system.

We then continue to act like school children, in a system designed to treat us like children… and if curiosity never re-emerges from the depth of our childhood psyche, we will spend the remainder of our busy lives as slaves, to a system we never knew existed.

We have been taught to believe we are "free", by a system designed to enslave us.

But, do you really want to know you are a slave? Is that something you want to add to your already stressed-out daily life? I have spent a lifetime trying to awaken this reality in the minds of my fellow human beings and came to the conclusion that most, simply don't want to know. It is a conscious choice, stem from the childhood psyche that cannot let go, and will never let go, due to the fact that no one has any idea of what to do about the situation.

This is where two worlds collide.

The Good Citizen

The good citizen/slave is so hopelessly misinformed and consumed by fear, that even the thought of public disobedience is an impossibility, due to the fact that they are completely unaware of their own enslavement.

The truth seekers, at many different levels, may come to understand their own serfdom, but blame the "sheeple" because they are unaware. So, they spend a great deal of time trying to "wake up" others to the reality of things, because they also have no idea what to do about the situation. Although informing people of the truth is certainly a step in the right direction, it is a futile endeavor when delivered to an unreceptive audience.

The system is ingeniously designed to send any truth seeker down the wrong path, and if any actually pursue the truth far enough, their quest will end at the zone of silence.

In reality, the actual solution is simple in concept. Everyone must join together, understand their situation and just say "no". The rulers have no power without our consent. They are outnumbered.

In any case, such a feat would require a means to unite the masses under one banner. However, due to the massive disunity caused by the varying levels of ideological tolerances amongst the populace, most will only support a leader that harbors their same beliefs and interpretations.

This unyielding particularity can also be used as a convincing argument to justify an unwillingness to act, and vindicate a timid position, as the truth seekers are just as fearful of taking action, as the people they mock.

FLASHBACK…

I was having a drink one evening in a local pub, sharing thoughts with a half dozen other like-minded individuals. All of us fully aware of the corrupt system and ready to condemn the majority for their ignorance and conformity.

Fate decided to test our resolve that night when the leader of the national opposition party at the time… candidate for Prime Minister in the coming national elections… Jack Layton (R.I.P.), walks into the pub. Perfect opportunity to share our concerns with a person of stature and influence. It is not often that one gets to have a personal conversation with the possible future Prime Minister.

I quickly turned to my fellow truth seekers to contemplate the best way to approach the man with our concerns.

To my disappointment, I had turned to face a group succumb to fear and unwilling to act. Eyes were turned downward and no one was prepared to approach him.

I however, was not going to let this opportunity pass, and proceeded to approach the man, which was standing next to the billiard tables, and introduced myself.

I expressed a few concerns regarding current situations at the time, such as the attacks of 9/11, and whether he would support an independent investigation into the true causes of this tragedy, to which he did agree, and then asked him a question that I knew he wouldn't answer. The purpose being, to see his reaction. If you pay close attention to someone's initial reaction when confronted with a serious question, you can easily assess their understanding of the question and immediately determine if they are being truthful in their reply.

I told him that it is common practice for the opposition party to oppose everything that the government in power proposes, but in reality, know they are just playing a game for their constituents to make it look like they are bringing a voice of concern and opposition to unpopular proposals, to fool the public into thinking they actually have a voice in parliament, all the while conspiring with the real power behind the government. I asked him if he was such a person.

Obviously, he was not going to answer "yes" to that question, but his reaction is all I needed. I thanked him for his time and went back to my table to share the experience. Out of the corner of my eye, I could see the honorable member periodically peeking over towards our table, trying to assess what had just happened.

(End of Flashback)

I realized at that moment, that if the people who are fully aware of the deception and have an understanding of the corrupt system cannot find the courage to act when given an opportunity, how then can we expect anyone else to act?

The bigger picture…

It was also at this moment that I started to recognize the bigger picture. It is well known and understood by the ruling oligarchy that the vast majority of the population will not question the system. There is a smaller percentage that will question the establishment but will never do anything to change their situation. They are led into the world of alternative media, designed to steer individuals in the direction of emotional reactionism and create a heightened sense of urgency towards affecting change. Accountability is directed at the un-aware citizenry and focus therefore, is aimed at "waking-up" the sleeping masses to the conspiracy.

The unaware have already been conditioned to fear these "dangerous conspiracy theorists" and will never entertain their rants. In this manner, a merry-go-round effect is created and nothing ever gets solved.

A smaller portion will actually be sufficiently motivated to take action. These are led by organizations which the system funds and controls for the purpose of making sure these people are never able to affect change.

Anyone who becomes a real threat are "taken care of" by the system by various methods. If a politician decides to act within his/her conscience and opposes a certain legislation, he/she will be disgraced on public television and the people will scorn them, not realizing that he/she was actually acting in their best interest.

Other methods require a more direct approach. The "ruling class" are evil in ways that most of us will never understand. They are willing and able to do anything for their cause of world domination, and despise anyone who might expose their deception. Human beings are cockroaches in their eyes and they feel no sympathy or remorse when leading millions to their death in wars, conflict, or economic collapses. Assassinations are just part of doing business.

Many will not believe there is a ruling class of people who control the world from behind the scene. They believe that it is too big to be true. But that is simply pure ignorance, as this fact is not hidden. All one needs to do is look. Their literature is found everywhere on the internet for us to see. They are all around us in our living rooms, class rooms, cubicles and vehicles. They are in the clothes we wear and the food we consume. They teach us how to think and how to react to certain situations. They teach us how to treat each other and how to speak. They are in our science and our history.

"For we are opposed around the world by a monolithic and ruthless conspiracy that relies primarily on covert means for expanding its sphere of influence – on infiltration instead of elections, on intimidation instead of free choice, on guerrillas by night instead of armies by day. It is a system which has conscripted vast human resources into the building of a tightly knit, highly efficient machine that combines military, diplomatic, intelligence, economic, scientific and political operations. Its preparations are concealed, not published. Its mistakes are buried, not headlined. Its dissenters are silenced, not praised. No expenditure is questioned, no rumor is printed, no secret is revealed."[12] – *John F. Kennedy – 35th President of the United States*

The following example serves to substantiate the premise of an independent, outside force manipulating the governments of different countries around the world, towards a common agenda.

After the attacks of 9/11, many countries were compelled to adopt anti-terrorist legislation. A perceptive YouTuber had noticed something particular and produced a video featuring then leader of the opposition party in Canada, Stephen Harper, making his speech to parliament regarding this subject, on March 20th, 2003. The screen was split with Harper, and the leader of the Australian opposition at the time, John Howard, producing the same speech word for word in the Australian legislature, on March 18th, 2003. The same text had been confidentially sent to both leaders, apparently believing that no one would notice.[13]

Why would such an important revelation not be shared on the evening news? Well, actually it did make the news. This video made such an impact that they were forced to recruit another political figure, Bob Rae, now Canada's ambassador to the U.N., to expose this questionable situation and demand answers from the opposition party.

As John Howard's speech was read two days before Harper's, the onus was on the Canadian Prime Minister to dissipate this obvious scandal. The only action necessary was for him to hold a press conference and admit that his writer had plagiarized the Australian leader's speech. The writer was fired and the whole incident was swept under the rug and never again cited.

Not one media personality dared contradict this excuse and question the validity of these claims. You need only distribute a good excuse through a "respected" platform and no one will question its authenticity.

Politicians are masters of oral manipulation… it is why they are politicians. But this power is only effective because of people's tendency to only hear what they want to hear.

I was watching footage from a Chamber of Commerce meeting in Winnipeg, Manitoba where then Premier Gary Doer was giving a speech to a packed house of businessmen, local politicians, environmentalist etc. There was a great deal of controversy at the time surrounding the destruction of large sections of land, caused by hydro-electric projects. Doer assured the businessmen that these projects were going forward, as the land surrounding the dams were uninhabited and useless. He proceeded to read his speech, and a few minutes later, proclaims that their government is dedicated to protecting the environment and the rights of aboriginal people, to ensure that their properties do not get destroyed by large hydro-electric projects.

The businessmen were happy that their large government contracts and investments were secure, and the environmentalists were assured that the government supported their cause.

The media however, is not there to point out this double speak. Coverage of the entire event must be condensed into a two-minute item, and must therefore be restricted in content. As the environmental concerns were an important subject at the time, news coverage focused on this issue. Government support of protecting aboriginal land could be substantiated in the reportage, by extracting a clip from Doer's speech where he says that his government is dedicated to ensuring the safety of the environment, and everyone would be led to believe that his government is supporting their cause.

The journalist was not sent to expose government support of large corporations, the story revolved around whether the government supported the environmental issues and aboriginal concerns. And although his government did support the continued development of hydroelectric projects in the area, it was also publicly stated that they supported the protection of the environment, and could therefore claim this position.

Doer was a master orator and proved his skills in front of Harper at a press conference regarding the North American Trade and Transportation Corridors initiative. Harper was not fully informed on many of the details and referred a journalist's quarry to Doer, which answered the questions regarding this subject with ease. Impressed, Harper congratulated him on his answer before going back up to the podium.

I remember mentioning to a journalist at the time that Doer would soon quit his position as Premier because Harper would offer him a better job. A few short months later, Doer announced that he had accepted an offer as Canada's ambassador to the US in Washington DC and was stepping down from his position as Premier of Manitoba.

Once you have an understanding of how the system functions, you can pick up on certain nuances, making it is easy to predict and unravel what goes unnoticed by the unsuspecting public that does not question the motives associated with such actions, as these political figures are trusted by the general population as men of stature and renown, stem from the media's ability to create such concepts.

Whether you are a politician, musician, actor, writer or hockey player, we can brandish your face on television and turn you into a star. It is a power I have yet to understand.

Idoltry is fantasy. The things you idolize are as deserving of this worship, as the things you do not.

We all have our role models that resonate with our particular predilections, helping to guide our actions towards our desired life's pursuits. It is important however, to recognize the distinctions between admiration and worship.

A man of renown came to our city one day and stationed himself inside a large local shopping center. Across the entire length of the mall and extending outside of the building, people were lined up to meet him. What did this man do to deserve such attention? He was an NHL hockey player.

Should we not consider that our infamous inventor, Philo Farnsworth, also deserve such admiration and worship? After all, he did invent the device responsible for the player's notoriety. It seems strange however, to consider idolizing Mr. Farnsworth, yet we can admire this inventor's accomplishments and its influence on our lives.

The hockey player can also be admired for his skill, determination, dedication, and the hard work required to achieve his success.

Both men are as deserving of our admiration, yet neither of them deserving of idolization.

As a sports celebrity, you are often seen on television and the media, which creates a sense of presence in people's lives which accentuates your celebrity status in society, and is intensified by the enormous salaries and benefits included in this position, as today's society correlates wealth with importance.

Money talks, it would seem.

Chapter 5

THE MIGHTY DOLLAR

Money… we work for it, beg for it, kill for it, die for it, and worship it like a god. How ironic, that we should put so much importance in something that has no value whatsoever.

Considering the vast influence of money on our lives, it is remarkable how little of the process of money creation is known, by the majority of the population.

In short, money comes into being through deposits, stem from borrowing. Every time an individual, corporation or government borrows money, an amount equal to the amount borrowed is injected into the system. Banks do not lend money they have stored in their vaults; they create that money out of thin air every time someone borrows money. The interest charged on these loans however, is not created. So, in order to keep the system functioning, money must be constantly borrowed into existence so that more can be injected into the system to keep up with the interest, which creates more interest, to the point where it will inevitably collapse. In this manner, the entire wealth of a nation can be stolen by the ones who control the money supply.

Consider this… all debt is sold on the market in various forms (mortgage-backed securities, asset backed securities, etc.), and this debt is owned by various corporations. It is within their contractual rights to be able to call in all debt whenever they feel it is necessary. Since there is not enough money in circulation to be able to pay the combined debt of the entire nation, those of us who are left without the funds, will have our assets seized by their rightful owners. If you are one of the few who is free from debt, or actually does have enough saved up to be able to cover your debts, you must also consider another problem… government debt.

Surpassing your personal debt is also municipal, provincial and federal debt, to which you are also liable. It is well within the law for governments to seize all private bank accounts in order to secure this debt.

There is absolutely no need for economic recessions and depressions. These are fabricated states, driven by a usury form of monetary system. By the simple volition of private bankers, our money supply can be drastically increased, causing inflation, or withdrawn from the economy, causing deflation.

I embarked on the journey to discover how our money system actually functions in Canada. I spoke to bank tellers, had a meeting with my bank manager, contacted the Credit Union Central of the province, the national and international governing bodies, contacted many politicians at all levels, and the foremost authority regarding money creation, Canada's central bank; the Bank of Canada.

The BoC does liberally document the underlying method of money creation on their website and in their literature. However, avoid divulging the fact that the interest charged is not created, which would obviously expose the fraud.

After considerable communications with the BoC, I was able to dissect their proper terminology and definitions, and formulate the right questions which would force them to admit the fraud. It was at this point that they told me they would no longer answer my questions… I had reached the zone of silence. It took me almost ten years to finally get them to admit that the interest is not created. Therefore, I now have definite proof of the fact that our money system in Canada is a fraud.

Here is a partial transcript of my conversations with the BoC.

From: …
Sent: November 18, 2011 12:14 PM
To: Public Information/Information Publique
Subject: RE: Money Creation

Thank you for your response. In 1939, the first Governor of the BoC made these statements to the Canadian Government's Committee on Banking and Commerce. Would you say that his statements are still relevant and accurate today?

"Q. But there is no question about it that banks create the medium of exchange?

Mr. Towers: That is right. That is what they are for... That is the Banking business, just in the same way that a steel plant makes steel.

The manufacturing process consists of making a pen-and-ink or typewriter entry on a card in a book. That is all.

Each and every time a bank makes a loan (or purchases securities), new bank credit is created — new deposits — brand new money.

Broadly speaking, all new money comes out of a Bank in the form of loans.

As loans are debts, then under the present system all money is debt

Q. When $1,000,000 worth of bonds is presented (by the government) to the bank, a million dollars of new money or the equivalent is created?

Mr. Towers: Yes.

Q. Is it a fact that a million dollars of new money is created?

Mr. Towers: That is right.

Q. Now, the same thing holds true when the municipality or the province goes to the bank?

Mr. Towers: Or an individual borrower.

Q. Or when a private person goes to a bank?

Mr. Towers: Yes.

Q. When I borrow $100 from the bank as a private citizen, the bank makes a bookkeeping entry, and there is a $100 increase in the deposits of that bank, in the total deposits of that bank?

Mr. Towers: Yes.

Q. Mr. Towers, when you allow the merchant banking system to issue bank deposits which, with the practice of using the cheques as we have it in vogue today, constitutes the medium of exchange upon which I think 95 per cent of our public and private business is transacted, you virtually allow the banks to issue an effective substitute for money, do you not?

Mr. Towers: The bank deposits are actual money in that sense, yes.

Q. In that sense they are actual money, but, as a matter of fact, they are not actual money but credit, bookkeeping accounts, which are used as a substitute for money?

Mr. Towers: Yes.

Q. Then we authorize the banks to issue a substitute for money?

Mr. Towers: Yes, I think that is a very fair statement of banking."

In other words, if I borrow money from a bank in Canada, they simply make an entry in a computer which increases their deposits by the amount borrowed and the BoC and the private banks create new money from that debt? The Canadian Bank Note Co. and BA International Inc. create money out of thin air while adding no value except for the medium of exchange used in the transaction?

Awaiting your reply,

René Normandeau

Dear M. Normandeau,

In response to your recent questions:

-       Would you say that his (Graham Towers') statements are still relevant and accurate today?

-       If I borrow money from a bank in Canada, they simply make an entry in a computer which increases their deposits by the amount borrowed and the BoC and the private banks create new money from that debt?

-       The Canadian Bank Note Co. and BA International Inc. create money out of thin air while adding no value except for the medium of exchange used in the transaction?

Here are our responses. I hope they are helpful.

-       With respect to Mr. Towers' explanation of how money is created in our economy, aka via commercial banks making loans, then yes, this comment remains accurate. The vast amount of money created in the economy is indeed created by banks by lending out, multiple times, the money Canadians deposit with them. Financial institutions can do this because they only hold as cash a fraction of the total amount of deposits held with them – generally they need to hold sufficient amounts to meet the day to day demands of their customers. This is how money is "created" in modern societies, and is called fractional reserve banking. I would add that the Bank of Canada can influence how fast the portion of the money supply created by financial institutions grows, by raising or lowering our policy interest rate, which then triggers adjustments in other lending and borrowing rates in the economy, making borrowing less or more affordable.

-       If you borrow money from a bank in Canada, that bank is lending you a portion of deposits it holds from other customers. If you deposit that loan with the same bank, then yes, it is registered as book-keeping entry in your account, and new money has been created from that loan. The other customers' deposits that the bank has used to make you the loan do not change, your deposits go up, so there is an increase in the overall money supply as a result of that transaction. Banks are able to do this because they know that it is unlikely that all their customers are going to walk into the bank at the same time and ask to withdraw all their money, hence the reason they only need to hold sufficient cash reserves on hand to service day to day customer needs.

-       Canadian Bank Note Co. and BA International are the two companies that the Bank of Canada uses to print Canada's currency. They supply a service to the Bank of Canada - they essentially print paper with coloured ink on it. Only when the Bank of Canada issues that paper into circulation does it become valuable. When we send new notes into circulation, the Banks that receive it in turn transfer the equivalent value in funds from their accounts to the Bank of Canada. So in the example of a $100 bill, they receive the $100 bill, and the Bank of Canada receives an increase of $100 in its own account, and the corresponding bank deducts $100 from its account at the Bank of Canada.

Our website has a wealth of information on these topics. I would suggest you take a look at the following explanatory backgrounders as well:

Sincerely,

…

Supervisor/Superviseure
Public Information Office/Service de l'information publique
Communications Department/Département des
Communications
Bank of Canada/Banque du Canada
234 Wellington, Ottawa, On, K1A 0G9
info@bankofcanada.ca

From: …
Sent: August 12, 2018 6:59 PM
To: Public Information/Information Publique
Subject: {External} interest

Hi, I was reading on your website that the money supply in Canada is created through loans and that deposits constitute the money supply. My question is, who creates the interest that banks and financial institutions charge on these loans? Is the interest created at the time of deposit?

Thanks

On 2018-08-15 10:04, Public Information/Information Publique wrote:

Good day,

Thank you for your email.

Commercial banks and other financial institutions are independent business entities that set their own interest rates for consumers; these are influenced by many factors, including the Bank's policy interest rate. It is also worth noting that the policy interest rate is the only rate the Bank of Canada has control over.

I hope you will find this information helpful.

Kind regards,

Public Information | Information publique
Communications
Bank of Canada
info@bank-banque-canada.ca

From: …
Sent: August 29, 2018 1:32 PM
To: Public Information/Information Publique
Subject: Re: {External} interest

Hi …,

Thanks for your reply. However, my question is not directed at the interest rates that banks charge but to the way the interest is created. From my understanding of how money is created in

Canada, money is only created through deposits stem from borrowing, but I am curious to know if the interest that banks charge on these loans is created as well because if the interest is not created then there would not be enough money in supply to actually pay for the interest of the combined loans in existence in the country today. Therefore, this is the question I am asking: Is the interest created? If yes, please explain to me how that is done. If no, just say "no, the interest is not created".

Thanks

Good day,

Thank you for clarifying your question, and our apologies for the delay in getting back to you.

The process of money creation can be illustrated with the following example:

Person A deposits $100 in a bank. The bank keeps $10 as reserves and to make a profit, and lends the remaining $90 to Customer B. Customer B spends the $90 by buying investments from Firm C, who then deposits the $90 with its bank. Firm C's bank keeps $9 as reserves and lends the remaining $81 to Customer D. If this chain continues indefinitely and 10% of the deposit is kept as reserves each time, in the end, an amount approximating $1,000 has gone into circulation and therefore become part of the total money supply.

However, in this process, the interest required by the bank is not created. An economy is able to repay the interest on the loans because its activity, which generates more revenues. For instance, Customer B described above will likely be able to repay the interest for its loan because it has made greater profits from its investment with Firm C, following the loan he contracted.

I hope this will help to further respond to your question.

Kind regards,

. . .

Public Information | Information publique
Communications
Bank of Canada

(End of transcript)

As we can clearly see from these transcripts, the Bank of Canada admits to the following:

1) "Money" is created from debt through private financial institutions.
2) "Currency" is not money, it is "paper with colored ink on it".
3) Deposits from loans injects new "money" into the money supply.
4) The interest charged on loans by private financial institutions is not created, therefore constitutes a fraud, as the combined loans cannot be fully re-paid.

These international "banksters" control the money supply of most nations around the world. This enables them to control the governments of these nations, which allows them to embezzle the entire wealth of the country, and impoverish its people. Add to the equation, a hegemony over the necessities of life, and you can create a world that is completely dependent on the system you've created.

Imagine that you were the first person to get a loan from a financial institution in this new type of banking system. You decide to borrow $2000 to build a shed. At the moment of deposit, $2000 dollars of brand-new Canadian money will have been created. A five-year term at 5% interest will accumulate $650.69 of interest by the end of the term. You now owe the bank $2650.69. But the bank has only created $2000 in Canadian money, making it impossible to pay back the loan. The bank will then proceed to seize the assets used to secure the loan, and will have gained real assets, without having provided any value.

However, if an entire society is borrowing money from the banks, there will be enough in circulation to make it possible over time, for an individual to pay back the loan. But if an entire nation would suddenly decide to pay all their loans at the same time… or financial institutions would call in all debt… there would not be enough money in circulation to pay the combined total.

At the moment, Canada is heading towards a state of hyper-inflation, as our money supply is being continuously increased by large amounts of debt, which generates an astounding amount of interest charges.

Canada's federal debt will soon reach approximately $2 Trillion dollars, accumulating at a rate of approximately $1000 per second, $86 Million per day, or $31 Billion per annum.

In other words, Canadians now owe hundreds of billions of dollars to private financial institutions that simply provide the country with a monetary system that could just as easily be administered by the Canadian Government, interest free.

A fiat money system is only made toxic through the charging of interest on loans. Money derives its value through our confidence in its worth. If a government issues its own money and accepts this "dollar" as payment for taxes, this money can be utilized as a method of trade amongst the population, assured of its worth. The money supply would be carefully monitored to remain stable with the amount of goods and services being traded in the country. Interest on loans would be abolished and replaced with a simple fee that would be added to the loan amount at the onset of the payment schedule, and the fee would be created and added to the money supply, thereby eliminating the cause of inflation.

What is inflation?

An economy is the combined total of all goods and services being traded.

Let's pretend that our dollar is based on the value of one chicken egg. If we have the equivalent of 12 eggs being traded in the economy, there should be $12 in circulation.

If the economy remains stable, but you inject another $12 into the system, you now have $24 in the system, yet only 12 eggs being traded. This is the sole cause of inflation, as every egg is now worth $2.

The egg has remained an egg, it has not increased in value, it is the money system that has lost value; therefore, you now need more money to pay for one egg.

Reversely, if you decrease the money supply to 6 dollars, you have created a state of deflation, as there is not enough money in circulation to accommodate the economy, which can create massive unemployment and depressions such the Great Depression of the 1930's.

The absurdity of adopting such a monetary system for your country confirms the treachery of the politicians involved, as no sane person would ever consider voting in favor of destroying their own country, were they not pressured by outside forces and agendas.

It is a grave misconception however, to believe that the goal of big business is money. The end game for these international bankers is not wealth... it is power. Money is only one of the means employed to accomplish their goals of world domination, and vital to this objective is the control of information.

If we can't place our trust within the most socially accepted sources of information, where then, can we find truth?

Chapter 6

ALTERNATIVE MEDIA

Before the introduction of the internet, alternative sources of information were mostly limited to written publications which were not always readily accessible. While television and radio did offer a seemingly alternative voice, its content was… and still is today… strictly regulated by the people who initially developed the technology as a tool to control information and promote their narrative.

The internet facilitated communication with such efficacy that anyone with the ability to connect to this electronic matrix could now reach a worldwide audience, comfortably sitting at home at a computer.

Such a platform had the potential of empowering a new generation of informed citizens, where corruption and secrecy could be efficiently exposed to the general public.

Of course, we cannot disregard the fact that the same people responsible for developing the most effective means of mind control ever devised… i.e. television and radio… were also responsible for creating the world wide web, and its true purpose is now becoming evident.

The new world order agenda is now reaching the final stages of completion, which is forcibly exposing the apparatus behind this diabolical scheme.

This envisioned future is of a world populated by a new kind of genetically modified human being, integrated with artificial intelligence, where we are grown in laboratories and exploited from birth, immutably connected to the matrix, where our entire lives are directed by artificial constructs and realities.

As this blueprint embodies the entirety of humanity, the internet had to be designed as a liberal network of expression in order to lure everyone into its web, and once adapted to this new system of communication, banking, socializing and shopping, this apparently free and open forum would be transformed into a censored control grid for the mind and body.

"Truth" will become a word with no meaning, in a dystopian nightmare disguised as a safe and secure "paradise".

Since the internet today is already heavily censored, where does one find "truth" in this maze of misinformation, misdirection and censorship? An extensive amount of research is essential to be able to maneuver through this labyrinth.

But what is "research".

We are all endowed with a natural curiosity for things unknown or mysterious. This irresistible appetite to solve mysteries and answer questions is the driving force behind all of creation.

After all, one cannot receive an answer, without first asking a question.

This natural curiosity is nowhere more evident than in the incessant questions cultivated in the minds of children, as they attempt to decipher their new and unfamiliar environment.

So powerful is this drive to answer questions, that this uncontrollable urge will sometimes compel one to fabricate replies for the sake of satisfying this inherent obligation.

Answers are inexorably linked to the quality of your questions, which are limited only by your level of understanding, which is determined by the extent to which you are able to open your mind to new ideologies.

Coupled with unyielding conviction, all quests will inevitably lead to the same conundrum… who are we and where do we come from?

Perhaps through indifference or fear of the unknown, you will limit your queries to modest pursuits and exist in a small world. Your reality can only reflect your limited perspective.

The ruling class have always used fear to discourage intellectual exploration, such as labelling information as "dangerous", or a "conspiracy theory", and creating a reluctance to investigate these subjects.

Journalists choose their words carefully when dealing with any information containing the slightest implication that it might be labeled a "conspiracy theory". Not because they are all "in" on the deception and are trying to hide something from the public, but because of the fear of the possibility that the viewing audience, or more importantly their profession, will believe that they support such "ridiculous" claims.

They will label a person "crazy", smirk, make a derogatory comment, shake their head, and use whatever body language they feel is necessary to ensure that their disbelief in these socially unaccepted topics is well communicated to the viewing audience.

When further confronted with the inability to debate certain facts, media personalities are obligated to use character assassinations as a last resort to convince the viewers that the information being presented by these "conspiracy theorists" is invalid, due to their mental health condition. They will even submit to government mandates that suggest that certain types of information are "dangerous" to public safety, and create enough fear in the general population to discourage any further inquiry.

How can journalists do their jobs, if the information that they should be presenting to their viewers is labelled as "dangerous" by their Federal Government?

There are however, many levels of "truth" in public perception.

Many alternative media sites reliably expose factual information and will usually back up their claims with credible evidence. But they will remain funneled on certain doctrines and limit their material to suit their vocation, and contain their beliefs within the boundaries set by their mind's acceptive tolerances.

Intermixed in this mess of misinformation and misdirection are agents of the establishment, there to instigate anger and mislead any sincere truth-seeker.

However, reliability does not signify trustworthiness.

There is a tactic used by mainstream media and politicians to bridge this gap, and simultaneously demonize opposition to their narrative and quell dissent. This ploy was clearly brought to light during the recent pandemic, as the drive to assure the populace of the safety and efficacy of vaccinations had been met with significant contradictory information.

In a desperate attempt to support their position, the media was obliged to draw on doctors, scientists and "experts", to reassure the public of the rightness of their claims, and vilify all opposing factual information and scientific data, by treating this information as "unreliable", as it did not originate from "trustworthy" sources. They would subsequently encourage their audience to avoid entertaining such "dangerous conspiracy theories", and applaud them as being astute intellectuals for blindly following their recommendations and not becoming imbeciles that are led astray and victimized by these "dangerous conspiracy theorists".

As most will not challenge any claims delivered on conventional media platforms, and are not informed beyond what they hear on the news, they are forced to consign their trust to what they have been led to believe are "trustworthy" sources of information.

Therefore, rather than researching both sides of the story and trusting the information itself, they validate the people… i.e. doctors, scientists and experts… and confidently accept their "expert" opinions.

The media will often demonize certain opposing views by associating these opinions with individuals that they have denigrated and/or characterized as conspiracy theorists. In order to avoid looking foolish, the public will dismiss the information being presented, strictly on the basis of the correlation made with these opinions, and the "crazy people" that are presenting the information.

As this method of coercing the public is so effective, it is common practice within the global establishment to hire individuals to support certain beliefs or "conspiracy theories", while purposefully expressing strong views on other socially unacceptable topics such as racism and holocaust denial, and let themselves be condemned by the media in a ploy to connect certain ideologies that are in no way correlated.

We can refer back to the Liberal Government utilizing the one man waving a flag adorned with a swastika at the trucker's rally in Ottawa, to demonize the entire group of protesters as Nazi supporters, and further associating free choice advocates with the same label, and to subsequently justify their fascist removal of the protesters and assure public obedience to their demands through fear of being labeled a racist Nazi, or of being arrested for disobeying their directives.

These tactics are utilized in both mainstream and alternative media platforms, and it's important that we base our decisions on the information being presented, and not the people presenting the information.

An extensive knowledge base is then necessary to fashion together the pieces of the puzzle and clarify the broader perspective.

This can only be accomplished by questioning everything through an unbiased mindset, directed towards an authentic pursuit of factual exclusivity.

Considering that this "ruling class" is fully aware of the fact that there are always those who will question everything, they have learned that it is in their best interest to create and fund institutions and organizations to expose and oppose their systems and agendas, in an effort to control the opposition, as this power enables them to lead individuals astray through subtle nuances in their data and deceptive messages, and virtually camouflage the truth within a labyrinth of mis-information.

Since there is such an immense diversity in the quantity and quality of research being performed by the general public, the confusion caused by this lack of intellectual clarity creates enormous discord and disharmony amongst the proponents of varying belief systems, not only limited to opposing paradigms, but extending to the varying edicts contained within the same creed.

The fight against the system has therefore become individuated and leaderless, and has created an immense cult of arm-chair warriors, hell-bent on creating change by sitting at home on their computers, expressing their discontent through various forums, and the comments section of articles and videos.

We can all sympathize however, as most of us are guilty of satisfying this need to express our dissatisfaction in this manner. Realistically, we are not left with many other options.

The fact remains however, that many alternative media sites have been initiated by well-meaning and intelligent researchers of all walks of life that felt the need to disclose their important knowledge to their fellow human beings.

Research however, should not solely be focused on media platforms, but also expand to any and all sources of information where pieces of the puzzle may be found. No individual can possibly have all the answers. There is simply not enough time in the life-span of a human being to be able to learn everything there is to learn. But a keen researcher may be able to access the life's work of many individuals, and connect their conclusions to a broader context, enabling them to solve problems that one who is focused primarily on his/her vocation may not be able to conceptualize.

For example: An American physicist by the name of Anthony Peratt, had been publicizing the high-energy plasma formations he was able to create in his laboratory, and his work caught the attention of David Talbott, a comparative mythologist, who had recognized that the plasma patterns being produced by Peratt looked identical to the ancient cave drawings that he was familiar with through his research, and decided to share his observations with Peratt.

Peratt was astounded to see carved on stone, the very patterns he had observed in his laboratory, postulating that these ancient artists may have been recording plasma discharge formations being produced in an age-old sky.[14]

This revelation prompted Peratt to begin studying the similarities between rock art drawings and his plasma formations, concluding that our ancestors must have been transcribing the patterns being produced by electrical plasma discharges in an ancient sky.

An unlikely connection, stem from two distinctive fields of study, made possible through communications technology.

Naturally, as with many other important discoveries, such innovative concepts do not align with our accepted "scientific" models, and are therefore, mostly ignored by conventional scientists, which serves to demonstrate the importance of alternative sources of information.

You will not find open-mindedness in our scientific community. Analogous to our journalists who are terrified of being ostracized from their profession by being labeled "conspiracy theorists", our skeptical scientists remain rigidly confined to their accepted ideologies for similar reasons.

Healthy skepticism is not without its merit, but may become a paradigm of its own, and be used as a front to conceal one's lack of understanding, or unwillingness to comprehend any concept beyond socially accepted boundaries. Many will come to identify themselves through this skepticism, and diagnose it as a measure of their intelligence, as it allows them to escape the possibility of being fooled or deceived by misinformation or lies. Generally, it is a fruitless approach to research and intellectual debate, which largely stems from a fear of being ridiculed.

Perpetual skeptics will never become the trailblazers to new ideas or concepts, and will deny themselves the freedom of discovering new truths, or the life-expanding revelations derived from any matter subject to faith.

There is a world beyond imagination to be discovered through alternative sites on the internet, and that is where you can find the means to unravel the true mysteries of this existence, and uncover the fraud that is disguised as "science" today.

Chapter 7

THE THEORY OF SCIENCE

It is both ironic, and an embarrassing fact, that many of our most widely accepted scientific "truths" are built entirely on theories.

They are affectionately labelled as "educated guesses", however, the fact remains that regardless of the amount of "education" supporting any theory, it is still lacking the support of verifiable evidence, and is therefore, merely well formulated speculation.

When reality does not measure up to proposed systems, mathematicians are forced to conjure up certain variables in their equations that do not reflect reality, but are a necessary component to their equation's functionality, which they will subsequently present as a working model to a mathematically illiterate public who will assume it is correct, as they have no alternative theory and are incapable of understanding the one proposed by the authorities in the field.

Nikola Tesla himself stated in the July edition of a science magazine published in the nineteen-thirties called "Modern Mechanix and Inventions", that mathematicians often use equations to build structures which have no connection to reality.[15] (p. 117-118)

If someone proposes an idea which contradicts your current doctrine, it should be greeted with an open mind, and engender a curiosity that leads to a better understanding of the subject in question. If you conclude that what you know is the only truth, and are not willing to entertain any information beyond this belief, you remain constrained to the levels to which your ego limits your paradigm.

How much of our sciences are based on guesses? The answer to this question must be met with sincerity, as most of us have been indoctrinated into believing theory as fact.

This is nowhere more evident than in the sciences supporting the theory of heliocentrism, and its lack of verifiable evidence has evoked a surge in the re-examination of geocentrism.

So controversial is this subject, that its mere mention is confronted with scorn and mockery. It is a prime example of our natural human tendency to adhere to popular common ideologies for the sake of feeling nestled and secure within a herd, or a group or society that will support each other in hateful condemnation of any who dare venture outside the walls of conformity and question the established doctrines.

However, as the theme of this discussion is to question everything, let us continue by investigating the sciences describing the environment in which we exist.

Consider this… If our model of the reality in which we live is false, and our knowledge and potential is limited to that conviction, then it follows that our understanding of the world could not grow beyond the reaches of this ideology.

Furthermore, when the vast majority of people have been led to regard themselves as the most intelligent and advanced society to have ever walked this earth, derived from their absolute confidence in their accepted model, the majority will fiercely defend their position for fear of ridicule and persecution… not to mention the shock of having to accept the fact that everything they've been taught and believed throughout their entire lives is a lie.

The following, are but a few examples of various scientific fields of study supporting heliocentrism, that are based on theories and/or mathematical equations that are built on assumptions.

Astro-physics
Astronomy
Evolution
Origins of the Species
Celestial Mechanics
Structure and Composition of Celestial Bodies
Big Bang
Relativity
Black Holes
Dark Matter

In fact, the entirety of these sciences lay upon the foundation of a single theory; the theory of gravity.

When Isaac Newton postulated his theory of gravity, he was forced to invent a new type of mathematics called fluxions, in an attempt to give credit to his ideas and convince his piers of its validity. This gave rise to calculus, which is based on numbers that cannot exist in the real number system, called infinitesimals, and became the foundation of modern mathematics. Albert Einstein also had to rely on mathematical concepts such as tensors, in an attempt to prove his theory of gravity.[16]

Tensors are mathematically derived objects that are used to describe physical properties. Tensor theory was introduced to Einstein by Marcel Grossmann, an expert in tensor calculus, who collaborated with Einstein to develop the Theory of General Relativity and the Theory of Gravitation.

There are in fact many different theories of gravity. Some expand on Newton's and Einstein's theories, and others propose alternative ideas, yet all have the same thing in common… they are guesses which attempt to support the idea of heliocentrism.

A guess however, is only required when no facts exist to prove your point, but may also be utilized as a necessary component to substantiate a lie or a hoax.

If no one can provide any evidence to uphold this concept, shouldn't we consider that this model is false?

Why do we continuously endeavor to "prove" this archetype, when none have ever been able to provide a single piece of evidence to corroborate this idea?

There is a court case from the state of Georgia, where a man named Zen Garcia offered a $15,000 prize to anyone who could prove the earths curvature, or prove that the earth had any movement more than fifty miles per hour.

William Thompson tried to claim the prize and was not able to provide enough evidence to convince the judge and lost the case.

How is this even possible?

If our sciences regarding this subject are infallible, why can't anyone provide enough evidence to convince a judge in a court of law? Shouldn't any University Professor, Astronomer or Astro-Physicist be able to easily win this prize?

From the moment we are born, we are inundated with sci-fi programs and movies, schooled on this model from kindergarten, shown beautiful images of earth from "space", as well as images of galaxies, nebulas, supernovas etc., in magazines and television programs, bombarded by NASA space missions featuring our famous "astronauts" performing space walks and mid-air spins in "zero G" during interviews from the "space station", and unquestionably become completely convinced of this reality.

But we cannot deny what can be seen with our own eyes… surely, we can't be suggesting that these organizations are involved in a massive hoax to undermine our understanding of the environment in which we live.

Logically, we must question the validity of the evidence provided to determine whether they are undeniable facts. Neglecting this process is unscientific and can only lead to ignorance.

Therefore, should we believe that images of earth from space and other objects in the universe that are produced by space agencies, be considered "hard evidence"?

The original Blue Marble photograph taken by the Appollo 17 mission in 1972 is claimed to be an actual photograph. It is unknown however, who actually took the photo, as all three astronauts on board, Eugene Cernan, Ron Evans, and Harrison Schmitt, claimed to have taken the photo.

However, the iconic Blue Marble picture produced in 2002… included as one of the default images on the early iPhone… is admittedly a composite photoshopped image.

Robert Simmon, the Senior Program Analyst from NASA who created the image, admits that there are very few actual photographs of earth from space, as all of NASA's earth-observing satellites are in low-earth orbit, and therefore, not far enough to capture the entire sphere in the lens of a camera. He created the famous picture using a composite of multiple 2,300 km wide strips of data, collected over four months by the Terra satellite as it orbited the earth. This data was then used to create a flat map of the earth, which was then wrapped around a sphere to create an image of an earth globe.[17, 18]

A post on the NASA website titled "History of the Blue Marble" states that the 2002 image is the most detailed, true-color image that they had ever produced at the time.[19]

However, Robert Simmon describes how the image was a product of his own imagination, detailing his vision of how the world would look like from space.

The first step was to remove all of the clouds. He then continued to change the color of the oceans, adding dark blues and greens in certain areas. He had to paint in the gaps between image strips, then add the clouds back in, often making use of the clone tool to copy and paste various cloud formations in different areas of the sky, and add a photoshop blur layer to simulate the atmosphere. He also had to add the specular highlight on the ocean. Of course, the black around the earth was simply a colored background, added to simulate the darkness of space. Considering the nature of the data received from the satellites, in order to produce a picture of the entire globe… as Robert says… it has to be photoshopped.[20]

A specular highlight is the bright spot that appears on a glossy object when illuminated by a bright light. At high altitudes above the earth, for example, you will be able to see a localized shiny reflection from the sun's light on the oceans.

Apart from the 1972 photograph, NASA does not claim to have published any authentic photographs of the earth, until the images produced by the Deep Space Climate Observatory in July of 2015. An animation was produced using actual satellite images, each being a composite of three separate exposures, to produce one final image. The animation was made using a series of images taken between 3:50 pm and 8:45 pm EDT, with the moon traversing the frame in the foreground.

Curiously, despite the fact that the images were taken over a period of almost five hours, there is virtually no observable movement of the clouds. From my own experience observing clouds move across the sky, I would expect that there would be a noticeable difference in the patterns detectable about every ten or fifteen minutes. Although many have tried to make sense of this unexplained phenomenon, none have provided any facts to substantiate their guesses, and it remains within reason to suspect that this animation is a computer-generated simulation.[21]

Can CGI and composite images be considered incontrovertible evidence?

We obviously cannot deny that the National Aeronautics and Space Administration exists. They have offices, thousands of employees, laboratories and research centers spread across the United States, and resources that permit them to develop and build incredible products, including various rockets and spacecrafts that we can witness being launched from the surface of the earth.

Considering the immensity of this organization, why should we question the authenticity of the images they provide? A more relevant question may be, why can they not provide enough evidence to prove their claims in a court of law?

We must also consider the viability of being able to deceive thousands of employees. However, their secrets could be held within a small percentage of employees that are given access to information on a need-to-know basis, and be limited only to those who would by necessity, have to be aware of the deception.

In reality, mission control has no way of knowing the difference between a simulation and the "real thing". After a space shuttle is launched and travels beyond physical visibility, everything associated with the flight becomes computer data and CGI. Mission control cannot differentiate reality from a simulation, and the general public's belief in these "space missions" are left entirely to faith.

In a book written by Appollo Flight Director Gene Kranz, he admits that the simulations were so real that no one could tell the difference between the training simulations and the real mission.[22]

It is akin to a large organization having immense resources such as ships, planes, snowmobiles, winter survival equipment, video equipment and communications technology, being able to physically prove their existence and technological resources to the general public, embarking on an Antarctic journey to the "edge of the world", while fully documenting their mission with real time video and audio feeds… then upon gaining close proximity to their planned destination, all video and photographic evidence to support their claims becomes photoshopped CGI… because it "has to be".

Should this photoshopped "evidence" be admitted as proof of their claims, simply because we can prove the existence of this organization and its technology?

In fact, Antarctica has been made inaccessible to the public by the Antarctic Treaty, signed in 1959 by twelve different countries, and came into force in 1961. Therefore, independent exploration of this land is prohibited by international law.

During the year when this treaty was signed, 30 wars, revolutions, coup d'états and other conflicts were being fought throughout the world, during which was the beginning of the third industrial revolution involving countries which were polluting the environment, destroying the forests and land for resources, slaughtering millions of animals to produce various products, over-fishing the oceans, testing nuclear weapons, and generally raping the world for profits without discretion.

Amidst all of this chaos, it was decided by international decree, that Antarctica… fifth largest continent in the world, brimming with natural resources, virtually defunct of flora or fauna, with a population of zero, would remain untouched. Maybe our leaders had a soft spot for penguins.

Wouldn't it be logical to mine our resources where it would have the least impact on the environment and our lives?

Wouldn't it be logical to allow independent exploration of this continent, and finally put to rest the controversy surrounding this question of our model of the earth? Furthermore, why does any organization or country believe that they have the right to deny any other person or country travel access to this part of the world?

We are given a host of environmental issues that seem to add up to a reasonable justification for restricting access to the continent, backed by mountains of scientific data produced by a well- funded scientific community, and sold this moral resolution through countless magazines, documentaries, and the media… which plays a key role by providing a platform for industry representatives and scientists to dazzle us with their techno-jargon and "scientifically proven data", which they utilize to authenticate doomsday scenarios and environmentalism, convincing the populace that such actions are necessary to "save the world".

When considering the fact that our scientists are responsible for causing more damage to the earth… and to humanity… than all natural disasters in recorded history combined, why do we still place the fate of humankind… and of earth… in the hands of the same industry that is liable for creating its problems?

Oddly enough, in the case of environmentalism, they have succeeded in convincing the populace that their own negligence is to blame. Common is this belief that "WE" are destroying the "planet", or that "WE" are polluting the air and causing "global warming". Although we cannot deny humanity's participation, it's important to clarify that this prefabricated society… i.e., our current dependence on hydro-electricity, petrol and silicon, was purposefully designed in this manner, and "WE" are literally forced to comply to this carefully planned techno-dependent social order.

Our "scientists" are bred through the system and emerge specialized in their respective fields of academia, producing mathematicians, physicists, chemists, geologists, biologists, astronomers etc., which are educated using a standardized curriculum, engineered by the very organizations that are hiding true knowledge from the public.

Virtually none of the students will question what they are taught, and will join the workforce as laboratory technicians and scientists performing routine tasks for large corporations and government organizations established for specific purposes.

Our new innovations and breakthrough technological advances are ideas that are funneled down from the very few at the top, where true knowledge and science is safely guarded, and where the standards for the whole are established.

Although we might like to believe that our local colleges and universities are bastions of research and innovation, we should also remember that virtually everyone we know in our scientific communities are simply trained employees who do not question the system, and therefore cannot be trusted as a source of true knowledge.

Let us examine a few of our well-known scientific beliefs.

The Big Bang Theory

This theory proposes that in the beginning, there was nothing. Somehow, this nothingness exploded. From this nothingness came something. Stem from the explosion of nothingness, this something was sent hurdling in all directions through something we call space, which arose from nothing. These objects had mass, which somehow developed an attraction to each other that we now call gravity. Throughout billions of years these objects with mass were attracted to each other (even though they are moving away from each other, stem from the initial explosion) and formed bodies with even more gravity. These objects started revolving around each other, somehow developing into stars, planets, radiation, light, sound, lava, trees, rocks, water, beings with legs, fur, lungs, blood, eyes, senses, digestive systems, neurological systems, mouths, fingers, brains, and at some point, some of these somethings developed the ability to actually contemplate their own existence and come up with theories such as this one, and manage to convince all the other somethings that they are complete idiots if they don't believe in this proposed system.

If we blew up the moon and sent its contents hurling throughout space in all directions, assuming that it was the only thing that existed in the universe, would its remains eventually start re-assembling themselves into worlds and start supporting vegetation and sentient beings?

Most religions around the world currently accept this model, yet source its inception as being created by God.

Let us examine this further.

All cultures that have existed throughout recorded history have all been proponents of the geocentric model, without exception. We have only recently converted our beliefs towards the heliocentric model.

At this point, I must point out the fact that the claim I just made is not a fact. Although some of our history can be substantiated with facts and historical artifacts, the fact remains that we cannot go back in time to prove the interpreted doctrines, and are therefore left to accept the popular beliefs, or consider alternative explanations. The fact is, that what we often believe are facts, are not facts, but interpretations and guesses, peddled as facts.

Therefore, by strictly adhering to a policy of factual exclusivity, let us examine some observable and measurable facts, and determine which model can stand up to scrutiny.

While observing a ship travelling away from your sight on a body of water, it would seem that the lower part of the ship begins to disappear below the horizon, until eventually the entire ship vanishes from sight. This phenomenon is still widely used today as evidence confirming the curvature of the earth, despite having already been proven false since the advent of the telescope.

The human eye perceives the world in such a way as to be able to judge distances. It is commonly known as the train track effect, whereas a person viewing parallel lines will notice that the lines seem to converge in the distance, yet it is simply an illusion caused by our method of perception.

We can quickly disprove that our ship is disappearing over the curvature of the earth by simply viewing it through a high-power optical zoom lens… at which point the bottom of the ship becomes once again visible… which of course would not be possible if it was being obscured by the bulge caused by the earth's curvature.

Heliocentrism requires that the surface of bodies of water curve at a rate which is proportional to the diameter of the sphere upon which it rests. We have the ability to calculate the size of the presumed hump between two points on a sphere, by using the Pythagorean Theorum equation of 8 inches per miles squared.

The following calculations are examples that should hold true to the earth, given a radius of 3959 miles.

Distance - Curvature

1 mile - 0.00013 miles – 0.67 feet
2 miles - 0.00051 miles – 2.67 feet
5 miles - 0.00316 miles – 16.67 feet
10 miles - 0.01263 miles – 66.69 feet
20 miles - 0.05052 miles – 266.75 feet
50 miles - 0.31575 miles – 1667.17 feet
100 miles - 1.26296 miles – 6668.41 feet

According to these calculations, if you stand on the shore of a lake which is 20 miles across, the water should have a bulge of approximately 266 feet between yourself and the shoreline on the other side of the lake. It would therefore be impossible to see anything on the other side which stood below 266 feet in height.

Why then do we have countless documented observations of objects being visible across long distances above bodies of water, which should not have been visible if the earth were a globe?

Let us expand on the example above, as there are certain variables to consider. The height of the observer would certainly have an impact on our numbers. Fortunately, we can calculate such factors in our equations.

By setting up our telescope on a tripod, with the lens resting at a height of 6 feet above water level, our calculations would then gauge the bulge at being 193 feet, making it still impossible to see anything lower than 193 feet in height.

We must yet add another variable to our equation, which is that of atmospheric refraction, whereas light waves traveling through the atmosphere will have a tendency to bend over long distances. The degree to which the light will bend is dependent on certain atmospheric conditions such as temperature, air density and humidity at varying heights in the atmosphere.

There are typically 2 types of refraction: Astronomical refraction, and terrestrial, or geodetic refraction. Astronomical refraction is virtually non-existent when observing objects vertically at 90 degrees above, and will increase as the observed objects are nearer the horizon, and its effects will become more significant when compared to terrestrial refraction as the viewed objects must travel through all layers of the atmosphere, whereas terrestrial refraction is limited to the lower troposphere.

As a side note, if you would like to learn where the different layers of our atmosphere actually begin and end, you will find yourself without a clear answer. Although it is commonly believed that the positions of these layers have been carefully delineated, the truth is that scientists have never accurately determined where they actually begin and where they end.

Terrestrial refraction is also affected by atmospheric conditions and is therefore subject to many variables, however the surveying community has established a standard atmospheric refraction index of $1/7^{th}$ that of curvature as a guideline.

Utilizing this as a basis for our calculations, we can adjust our numbers as follows: 266' of curvature divided by 7 equals 38'. Subtracting this amount from 193' still leaves us with a substantial bulge of 155'. Therefore, nothing below 155' should be visible across the lake at a distance of 20 miles, from an observation height of 6 feet.

As this is just an example, I have compiled a short list of actual documented observations from various distances, testifying to the fact that in the physical world, the bulge of the earth simply cannot be detected.

The following examples were calculated, accounting for the height of the observer and the standard refraction index, and are listed as follows: Location, Observed target and its height, Height from the bulge of the earth that should be present between the target and the observer, Distance from the observer to the target.

Rock Lake, Manitoba – Light source, 12" – 5' bulge – 8 miles

Great Salt Lake, Utah – Laser light, 5' – 32' bulge – 21 miles

Cape Bonavista, Newfoundland – Lighthouse, 150' – 420' bulge – 35 miles

Isle of Wight, England – Lighthouse, 180' – 854' bulge – 42 miles

Cape L'Agulhas – Lighthouse, 238' – 854' bulge – 50 miles

New York – Statue of Liberty, 305' – 1778' bulge – 60 miles

Genoa, Italy – Island of Elba, 3343' – bulge 7526' – 125 miles

It has been, and can be repeatedly demonstrated, that while utilizing scientific methods of observation and experimentation, calculating the distance from an observer to the target source being viewed, as well as the height of the observer above sea level, and allowing for refraction of light, no curvature can be observed or shown to exist.

Mount Capanne, the highest peak on the Island of Elba, stands at an elevation of 3343 feet above sea level. Although photographed from a distance of 125 miles, the entire island is clearly visible, despite the fact that its highest peak should be hidden behind 4183 feet of curvature.

In 2015, a famous photograph taken of the Chicago skyline by Joshua Nowicki, from across Lake Michigan at a distance of sixty miles, made such an impact that it to be addressed on the evening news, as the entire city should have been hidden behind over 2000 feet of curvature, exceeding the height of the tallest building in the city by over 500 feet. The meteorologist on the local newscast quickly dissipated the public's bewilderment associated with this impossible photograph, by quoting the given "scientific explanation" that attributed the cause as being a mirage.

For the sake of context, let us hypothesize that a photographer had climbed up a 200-foot tower on the Michigan side and had taken a photograph of the Chicago skyline across Lake Michigan, and the only thing visible in the photograph was the top 200 feet of the 1451-foot Willis Tower, clearly demonstrating a measurable bulge caused by the curvature of the earth. Let us further hypothesize that our scientific community believed the earth to be completely flat, and confronted with this evidence, concluded that the reason that the entire skyline could not be seen was due to atmospheric conditions that caused the light to bend downwards towards the water, giving the illusion that there was a bulge between the photographer and the city of Chicago across Lake Michigan. Although several other experiments were conducted over bodies of water under various atmospheric conditions and various distances which clearly demonstrated a bulge between the observer and the object being viewed, the scientific community still maintained that their explanations were indeed valid, and added that the proponents of the ball earth were simply fools who were misguided by dangerous conspiracy theorists.

Should we trust a scientific community that uses illusions and mirages, theories, lies, computer generated imagery, computer generated models and name calling of anyone who questions their models and ideologies as the foundational structure of their scientific doctrines?

Although I do not question the existence of mirages, as I have personally witnessed this phenomenon across Great Slave Lake in the Northwest Territories in Canada, I do question its use as a "go to" without actual evidence, to describe "unexplainable" phenomena. I will also add that the mirage that I witnessed produced a reversed image of the horizon, separated and floating above the horizon. It did not elevate and reproduce a clear image of what should have been hidden behind the horizon.

It is imperative that we question and examine the evidence profusely, yet must also consider the source of such scientific ideologies, and the motives driving this indoctrination. We shall cover this topic in the following chapter.

Most however, are so completely sold on the idea of heliocentrism, that it sounds absurd to even question something that is so commonly known and accepted as a fact.

It is now also commonly known that the air we breathe and cow farts are "killing" the "planet". At first glance, such a proposition does not inspire confidence, but call it CO_2 emissions and methane gas pollution, and these scientific connotations magically generate plausibility.

However, we might be relieved to learn that our clever scientific community has developed a feed additive called Bovaer®, that can help to eliminate 30% of cow burps, in order to reduce the harmful effects of belching on the climate.

We can expand beyond either of these models however, and entertain even more interesting descriptions of our reality.

Holographic Theory

The Holographic Theory, or Holomovement as coined by David Bohm, a Quantum Physicist from Pennsylvania, suggests that the three-dimensional world we perceive with our eyes, is actually encoded on a two-dimensional surface.

A hologram is created by bouncing a beam of light (laser) onto an object that you want to reproduce as a hologram, and another beam of light directly onto a special photographic plate. The two beams will interact with each other and create an interference pattern across the plate. To the naked eye, the patterns form an incoherent image, but shining a laser beam through the plate will create a 3D image.

Large amounts of information can be stored on a single plate, as shining the laser beam at different angles will produce different images. Furthermore, if the film is cut into several small sections, the whole of the image will still remain in every individual piece, and the entire hologram can still be reproduced by shining the beam through just one of the pieces.

Holography was invented by Dennis Gabor, an engineer and physicist who developed the hologram as a means to improve the image quality of electron microscopes.

His work with electron beams also led him to invent a flat screen television using a cathode ray tube electron gun placed in a perpendicular position relative to the screen.

Expanding on Gabors theories, physicist David Bohm and neuroscientist Karl Pribram formulated the Pribram-Bohm holoflux theory of consciousness, showing that our physical reality actually stems from a deeper level of existence that works much in the same way as a hologram.

They postulated that we are all connected to an interwoven two-dimensional plane which contains the whole of consciousness, and is the source of our physical three-dimensional experience, such as the lasers that are reflected on a two-dimensional surface producing a 3D image.

This would suggest that the world outside of ourselves is not something we exist in, but something that is projected from within ourselves.

Experiments conducted by Pribram and others have shown that removing parts of the brain does not affect brain functionality or memory. This protective, non-local, holographic type of memory storage, allows the brain to maintain functionality even after having suffered injury or damage. Memory loss only occurs when there are no parts remaining that are sufficiently large enough to contain the whole.

It was also discovered that the brain cannot tell the difference between the holograms used to experience reality, and the world that is imagined in the mind, leading to the conclusion that at some level, we all possess the ability to shape our physical reality, by simply imagining it to exist in the manner in which we desire to see it manifest in our physical reality.

Such revelations are now helping to corroborate the ancient mystic philosophies that assess the world as being an illusion that mirrors back our inner thoughts and beliefs.

Not unlike a hologram that can produce different images depending on the angle at which the laser shines on the photographic plate, Bohm found that memories are stored in the brain in the same criss-cross pattern as the holographic plate, and reality is expressed according to our angle of perception.[23, 24]

The brain contains the whole of universal knowledge, yet with a limited perspective that allows us to be able to have a seemingly separate, individual experience within the whole.

If you observe an object in the physical world, this object exists in multi-dimensional form, and what we are seeing is a cross section of the object which is relative to the angle of consciousness, or dimension from which we perceive reality.

These revelations may therefore bring clarity to the methods used to manifest our desires, such as the Law of Attraction and the Law of Assumption, which require an individual to not only formulate a vivid image of their desired life, but to relax into a knowing that this wish has already been fulfilled.

A strong inner spiritual awareness and a focused mind, can not only produce tangible results in our everyday lives, but provide us with ability to alter and affect the physical properties of the world, and of our bodies.

We can gain some perspective on these theories when looking at the world at an atomic level.

We are all familiar with the standard model of the atom depicting a nucleus made up of protons and neutrons, with electrons orbiting the nucleus in a manner similar to the depiction of the planets of our solar system orbiting the sun.

This model is false however. Truth is that no one can tell you what an atom looks like because it has never actually been observed. Electron microscopes only produce an interpretation of what it may look like, not an actual photograph of the atom.

An electron is more closely described as a wave of probabilities with no fixed location, and will collapse into a particle of existence when given direction by the mind. We can therefore correlate this quantum behavior of electrons to our ability to create our own realities.

The word "quantum" is a term used in physics to describe quantifiable levels.

You may for example, go into your kitchen cupboard and place a cup on one of the shelves, yet will not be able to place the cup between the shelves. In a similar manner, an electron can exist at various energy levels/shelves within an atom. Mysteriously however, if provided with a surge of energy, an electron can be made to instantly jump from one level to another, creating a "quantum leap". It is as though the electron disappeared out of existence, only to re-materialize in a different position.

Perhaps the electron is not popping in and out of existence, but merely reverting back to its two-dimensional form… where it would be unperceivable to us… and re-emerging back into the three-dimensional world where we can experience it in tangible form, utilizing the senses that we possess to experience this reality.

The mystics say that our world and everything in it is in constant motion. We can extrapolate from this concept and say that everything is a wave that is in constant vibration, and the frequency of vibration determines its qualitative features.

Glass, steel, wood, hair, skin, rubber, plastic etc., all vibrate at different frequencies that determine their respective attributes.

Sound therefore, seems to be the catalyst upon which everything in this 3D world is created, and allows us to interpret in a new light, our stories of creation that state that in the beginning, the world was created by sound, or the word, or the sacred song.

The science of sound, or cymatics, offers a glimpse at the intricate patterns produced by sound waves. By placing a fine sand inside a of a plate attached to a speaker and playing various sine waves from an oscillator, the sand will shape itself into beautiful geometrical patterns which are different for every frequency.

We may look at these different patterns of sound as the molds of physical objects in our 3D world.

According to Nikola tesla, even radio waves are sound waves in the air, asserting that his radio transmitters are but emitting sound waves in the ether. He also believed that everyone is linked by invisible forces.

Nikola Tesla (1856-1943) was a scientist and inventor who is considered the father of modern technology. He held approximately 300 patents, and his inventions include AC (alternating current) power, hydroelectric power, the Tesla coil, the Tesla turbine, the induction motor, neon lights, the transistor, the shadowgraph (X-rays), radio, the radar, wireless communication, remote controls and the laser, to name a few.

Some of his most notable inventions however, were sadly never adopted into the technological make up of this new world, and eventually became the source of his supposed downfall. Free energy devices such as the Magnifying Transmitter, which could wirelessly transmit electrical currents, was not popular amongst his financiers, determined to establish a society based on profit and control.

He had proven this technology by wirelessly powering light bulbs, and had built the impressive Wardencliff Tower in New York to demonstrate his new technology to the entire world, but at the cusp of this breakthrough, J.P. Morgan, the man responsible for financing his endeavors, pulled funding on the operation, which eventually forced Tesla into the shadows where he apparently died alone and penniless.

Tesla also suggested that the human mind could be controlled electronically, such as is being done today by DARPA's N3 program.

I must however, point out the shear ignorance of a scientific community that mocks a part of his work as scientific quackery, while utilizing the very technology invented by this man to not only belittle his most marvelous of achievements, but also enjoy as the basis of an entire way of life.

There are certain anomalies surrounding Nikola Tesla and his technology which deserve further scrutinization, however the context of this discussion must first be established, and will therefore be continued in chapter 9.

Questioning our most commonly held beliefs and entertaining alternative viewpoints, withholding a reverence towards authentic scientific pursuits and impartial analysis of all available data and experimental observations, withdrawing the need to strictly adhere to egotistical convictions for the sake of emotional security, is the only true scientific method.

Rejecting information simply because of a fear of having your beliefs being proven wrong is a path to ignorance and oppression, and affirms its own falsity, as it is the only way to maintain adherence to false doctrines and pseudo-science.

Our scientific community has built an entire model of reality, by accepting guesses and assumptions as being factual.

The phrase *"We know that…"*, or the even more comical *"What we think we know is that…"* undoubtably represents the foundation of modern astronomy, cosmology and astrophysics.

For example…

If you want to know the speed at which the earth revolves around the sun, you must first determine the distance that the earth travels in its orbit. In order to calculate the orbital length, you must first know the distance between the sun and the earth. *We know that* the distance is 43,955,807 miles. Using this measurement, we can clock the orbital speed at approximately 167,000 miles per hour.

If you want to calculate the distance between the sun and the earth, you must first know the speed at which the earth is travelling so that you may calculate the distance between two points over time in order to perform geometric calculations using parallax. *We know that* the earth travels at 167,000 miles per hour, so we can perform our calculations and determine its distance. The same method may be used to determine the distances of stars.

It is apparent that we are left with the proverbial, chicken and the egg conundrum.

Some of you might have noticed the errors in the above calculations. In actual fact, the distance between the sun and the earth is said to be 92,955,807 miles and the orbital speed approximately 67,000 miles per hour. These errors were intentionally placed to show that most of us cannot conceive of such distances and speeds of travel, and if we also cannot understand most of the science supporting these assumptions, then scientists have it in their power to convince us of virtually anything.

If I were to estimate the distance between Calgary, Alberta and Winnipeg, Manitoba at 14,000 miles, most of us could not be fooled. Our experience and knowledge would easily dismiss such a foolish claim, and the distance could be easily proven. But astronomical units and parsecs are to the majority, not within the realms of conceivability, and therefore, pseudo-science can easily be peddled as fact.

At present, we are born into this reality and accept this mundane existence as "normal", as we have no reference to a better system. The freedom enjoyed by the ruling class is something most of us cannot even comprehend.

We however, have been conditioned by Hollywood that being gifted or endowed with super powers is a great burden that we would gladly give up for a chance at a "normal" life… to have a job and raise a family, like everyone else.

I cannot fathom why anyone would give up their power of invincibility for a life of mediocrity, scarcity, low wages, stress, mortgage payments, bills and being hounded by collection agencies, yet isn't this what we have adopted as a "normal" life?

In a panel discussion titled "Ultimate Revolution" held at UC Berkley in 1962, famous writer Aldous Huxley stated that the ruling oligarchy were developing techniques to get people to enjoy a sub-standard way of life, and to actually love their servitude.[25]

"Through clever and constant application of propaganda, people can be made to see paradise as hell, and also the other way round, to consider the most wretched sort of life as paradise."[26] – *Adolf Hitler*

Most of us are quite happy leading a simple life, which is certainly an honorable endeavor, yet quality of life could be significantly improved, and hardships considerably lessened, given a society driven by truth and love, rather than servitude and ignorance.

Let us continue with an examination of another important and trusted field of science.

Health Care

Most of us are quite convinced that our modern health care system is near infallible. Technological innovations have provided better methods of diagnosing problems, and now enable surgeons to operate on the human body with much less invasive procedures. We can substitute limbs and organs with synthetically produced replacements, and we are quickly migrating towards the use of products being introduced in the fields of bio-engineering and nano-technology.

Pharmaceutical companies have created a pill for every ail and a vaccine for every virus.

We must question however, the validity of our marvelous medical system when considering the fact that we now have more heart disease, cancers, respiratory illnesses, deformities and allergies than in all of history.

Scientific papers like to boast of new developments in the treatment of this and that ailment, suggesting that they are on the path to discovering new cures for a variety of illnesses. This well-funded scientific community however, has yet to produce a "cure" for anything whatsoever, and instead flaunt the efficacy of their "treatments", which often cause more harm than good, and coincidently creates an enormous market for an endless variety of health care products and pharmaceutical drugs, which are "regulated" by organizations such as the FDA and Health Canada, and supported by companies such as the CDC.

We cannot dismiss the benefits of having a medical system capable of treating broken bones and other physical problems, and of the merits of certain medical products, for which I am grateful. However, a closer examination of our current academically accepted biological sciences, reveal flaws that have been purposefully injected to covertly conceal the true nature and fundamental architecture of certain physiological systems.

Such corruption can lead to the creation of an entire biological system, based on a single distortion of the truth, where the treatment of symptoms become the only option, as an understanding of the essential construct of the biological system in question is required in order to develop methods to remove the conditions causing the dis-ease.

The following examples will help to illustrate this point.

Germ Theory

The germ theory of disease became popularized in the 19th century through the work of Robert Koch and more famously, the father of immunology; Louis Pasteur… also responsible for the introduction of the process of pasteurization.

Observing the number of people around the world blindly following government orders to inject toxins in their blood stream and wear masks for protection against airborne pathogens, I believe it is safe to assume that most of us are convinced of the existence and dangers of what are labeled "viruses".

What if we were to question the existence of viruses?

The germ theory of disease was not so readily accepted by many doctors and scientists at the time of its inception, notably, French organic chemist; Antoine Béchamp, fierce opponent of germ theory.

Through his work and experimentation, Béchamp was able to prove that the mould from fermentation contained living organisms he called microzymas.

He found that these microzymas, or "little bodies", were present in all organic matter, including healthy or diseased tissue, and were essential to cell growth and repair.

After exhaustive studies and countless laboratory experiments conducted with his assistant Professor Estor, they concluded that rather than the cell, it is the microzymas that are the elementary building blocks of life.

In a healthy terrain upon which it feeds, grows and multiplies, the microzymas will develop into normal cells of the animal, vegetable or human organism. However, in an unhealthy environment, they will evolve into bacteria.

Bacteria cannot attack healthy tissue, its function is to rebuild diseased or dead tissue, and process waste materials such as sewage. It is not the cause of disease, but a result of a diseased condition.

We must remember that Antoine Béchamp was one of France's most notable scientists. He was a doctor of medicine and a professor of biological and medical chemistry, toxicology and physics. His accomplishments were so numerous that it apparently took eight pages of a scientific journal to list all his achievements.

His revolutionary work however, has been virtually omitted from our modern academic literature, and this mass censorship continues to this day with any and all who dare question the established germ theory of disease. The numerous scientists of his time, and countless scientists and medical doctors today, have been silenced by modern academia, the media and the internet.

Dr. Thomas Cowan, an outspoken medical doctor who refutes the germ theory of disease, was forced to surrender his medical license to California's medical board for spreading "misinformation" about Covid-19.

This type of fascist behavior has now become the new normal, and the majority of the population have been convinced that the mainstream scientific consensus is reliable and trustworthy.

I remember watching footage of an anti-lockdown rally that was being covered by an alternative news site in a particular Australian city, and the host walked up to a man watching the protest and asked him if he believed in their cause and he answered "no, I believe in science".

However, if this man truly believed in science, he would have joined the demonstrators, as the fact remains that viruses have never been proven to exist by the scientific community. In an attempt to distract the public from this fact, doctors and scientists will refer to the numerous experiments that have been conducted, purporting to have isolated viruses. But a closer examination of the methods used to "isolate" these viruses, exposes the deceptiveness of these claims.

Dr. Cowan admitted in an interview that in the entire history of published medical research, no virus has ever been found, including SARS CoV-2, HIV, Ebola and Zika.[27]

He has personally read over two-hundred papers regarding the isolation of a virus, and explains the process as such: They take the fluid of a sick person and filter it, then mix it with nephrotoxic antibiotics such as gentamicin and amphotericin, mix that with fetal calf serum and inoculate it on monkey kidney cells. Once the cells break down, the particles observed are then claimed to be the virus. The experiment was repeated without using fluid from a sick person and the cells broke down in the exact same manner, proving that the isolation is false.[27]

In an article published in the German SciencePlus (Wissenschafftplus) magazine, Dr. Stephan Lanka, a German virologist, reveals the dubious methods used by scientists, in an attempt to prove the existence of viruses, and the seven arguments used to refute their claims, adding that any virologist claiming that viruses are the cause of disease are fraudsters that should be prosecuted.[28]

The double-speak employed by politicians and journalists is quite evident, as no government or health agency worldwide has yet to provide any documentation proving that viruses have indeed been isolated. Although, the word "isolation" may have been re-defined to suit their needs.

A collection of Freedom of Information requests seeking records proving the isolation/purification of the COVID-19 virus submitted by various people around the world have been collected and published on the fluoridefreepeel.ca website.[29]

They have so far collected 220 FOI requests from 40 different countries, and not a single institution has provided proof of the isolation/purification of this virus.

It is stated on the website that after reviewing numerous responses, they determined that the word "isolation" in virology has been re-defined to mean the opposite of its definition in plain English.

This is a method often used by organizations, politicians and governments to lie to the public without actually lying. They simply define words to suit their specific needs, within acts of legislation, without divulging their true meaning to the public, and can confidently deceive, knowing that they are actually telling the "truth".

In other words, the scientific and medical establishments, as well as governments and media, will fiercely defend their position that viruses have indeed been isolated, and will viciously slander any who disagree with their analyses as unscientific conspiracy theorists spreading false information, yet when asked to prove their claims, cannot provide a single documented case of the isolation of a virus.

The PCR test which is widely used today, and venerated by media as the "gold standard" test for determining infection by a virus, was never created for such purposes, which is confirmed by the actual inventor, Kary Mullis, a biochemist who received the Nobel Prize for his invention. He stated on a panel discussion that Polymerase Chain Reaction is just a process used to amplify DNA molecules, it cannot determine the causes of sickness or disease.[30]

Kary also worked extensively in HIV testing and for a time he was working for Specialty Labs setting up tests to look for HIV in the blood supply of the city of Los Angeles, California, and had to write a paper for the National Institute of Health regarding the subject, to validate the necessity of funding the ongoing process of monitoring the blood supply for possible contamination.

His first objective was to demonstrate that HIV was the probable cause of AIDS, yet was not able to find any scientific documents to support this statement.

Kary was often required to demonstrate his PCR test, and therefore travelled extensively and met numerous people who were studying AIDS, so he decided to take advantage of the opportunity and ask them if they could provide him with a scientific document that he could quote for his paper. To his dismay, not a single one was able to help him with his query.

He then decided to change his approach and started to ask his colleagues at what point they had made the conclusion that HIV was the cause of AIDS, to which they could only point to news articles and television media.

However, he was convinced that he would be able to get his answer when he attended the grand opening of a new AIDS research center in San Diego, where famous French virologist Dr. Luc Montagnier, was also in attendance.

Dr. Montagnier was the recipient of a Noble Prize for having discovered that the HIV virus was the cause of AIDS. As the number one authority on the subject, surely he would be able to provide him with the documents he needed to complete his paper.

Montagnier suggested two different papers from which he could quote, and walked away from the conversation, leaving Kary defeated, as he had already read these papers and determined that they had nothing to do with HIV.

Interesting to note that Montagnier later stated that he felt it was against the public interest for governments to mandate vaccinations that had not been proven to stop the spread of the pathogen.[31]

Sadly, Kary Mullis was murd… excuse me… passed away in 2019.

Time and time again in the annals of science, there are assertions made that are taught as facts, yet upon closer examination are exposed as fabrications, and the root cause of sickness and disease is no exception.

We are being systematically poisoned by a host of chemicals and drugs meant to weaken our minds and bodies and destroy our spiritual connection, and an entire medical system has been fabricated to cover up this con against humanity.

They concocted "viruses" as the culprit behind the innumerable reactions to these poisons. They devised an "immune system" to support Germ Theory, and created imaginary biological systems to support their "treatments" of these conditions, and invented anatomical structures such as the "blood-brain barrier" to deceive people into believing that our brain is protected from certain drugs that could be harmful to its function.

A more in-depth analyses uncovers even more dubious historical facts surrounding germ theory. It would seem that Pasteur's notoriety is misplaced.

"Athanasius Kircher and Louis Pasteur financed by the Chigi-Albani Black Nobility family created "Germ Theory", a deadly, misguided teaching largely responsible for the spread of Bubonic Plague, 1918 Plague and Coronavirus today. In fact, no "Viruses" have been Isolated and proven to be the cause of any disease including HIV, Measles, Polio, HPV, Ebola, Zika, XMRV, SARS CoV (2003 "Bird Flu), MERS or the Common Cold. Hygiene, clean water/food promote health, not Masks and Vaccines; Disease is caused by the introduction of Pathogens via pollution and vaccination."[32]

A German journalist by the name of Samuel Eckert, has offered a guaranteed reward of 1.5 million Euros to anyone who can provide proof of the isolation of the Covid 19 virus. Surprisingly, no one has yet claimed this prize.

We have government tent agents, journalists, talk show hosts, virologists, medical doctors and "experts" in various fields, assuring the public that it is an undeniable fact that a deadly virus called SARS CoV-2 was the cause of the latest pandemic and is responsible for the deaths of thousands of people, yet not a single one of them has even attempted to claim this prize?

In other words, there exists no evidence to support Germ Theory, as viruses have never actually been isolated.

The purpose of such a deception may seem obscure, until you consider the possible motives.

United Nations Agenda 21 is a blueprint for human depopulation, and this culling of the human race is advocated as the most effective method available to decrease environmental degradation. Selective extermination could certainly be accomplished through the sadistic use of poisonous cocktails injected directly into our bloodstreams.

Sold as protection against disease, vaccines are ironically one of the most effective means for mass murder ever devised. The recent push to vaccinate the entire population against the "coronavirus" may now have resulted in an untold number of people carrying foreign substances in their bodies, with undetermined biological ramifications.

Untold numbers of people have experienced horrible adverse reactions and even death, just a few minutes to a few days after inoculation. Since its administration, we are now seeing an unprecedented increase in unexplained health conditions and cardiac arrests amongst adults of all ages, and most alarmingly in the younger generations, where such occurrences were previously almost non-existent.

It would seem that since the introduction of vaccines, countless medical conditions and deaths have been attributed to unknown causes. Is there a correlation?

The leading cause of death amongst infants is "Sudden Infant Death Syndrome" (SIDS)… in other words, the leading cause of death amongst infants today… is unknown!

Considering the boundless faith we have placed in our medical establishments, shouldn't we all be horrified at such a statement? Shouldn't our scientific community be ashamed of such a fact?

As an example: For no apparent reason, a young infant boy suddenly passes away in his sleep. A medical examiner proceeds to determine the cause of death. The logical approach is to investigate the anomalies which might have occurred during the preceding days before the incident. The child was well fed, happy, clean, well taken care of and in perfect health. In fact, the only deviation from normal in the child's life came in the form of an inoculation received just a few hours before death. Since vaccinations had already been "proven safe" by the scientific community, this evidence was deemed inadmissible, and therefore, the only option was to conclude that the cause is "unknown". Considering the fact that this anomaly has become the leading cause of death amongst infants, and the medical establishment cannot provide any answers, it was determined that they should give it a scientific sounding name to impersonate competency within the scientific community… in other words, the scientific consensus is that… "unfortunately, we have to accept that young infants die for no reason, hours after receiving an inoculation … these things happen."

Now imagine that an infant was terminally ill, and a few hours after receiving an inoculation, the child fully recovers and is cured. Upon investigation, it was determined that the only change in the child's daily routine was the inoculation. If the scientific community had established that vaccines could not possibly cure any child from any disease, should we now consider that the child just miraculously recovered, and proceed to conceal this cure from the public? The medical community could give it a good name such as "Sudden Infant Recovery Syndrome", and fool the public into believing in miracles.

Today, after this massive vaccination campaign, our young adults are having heart failures at unprecedented rates, and the dumbfounded medical establishment has to rule out vaccinations as a cause because once again, it has been established that these pharmaceutical products are safe and effective and cannot be considered as a cause. Therefore, the medical community decided to adopt a new scientific name for this perplexing condition… "Sudden Adult Death Syndrome" (SADS).

At this point, I should like to use a completely outrageous sarcastic remark as an analogy to illustrate the absurdity of this "scientific diagnosis", but nothing more ridiculous comes to mind.

Curing heart disease may prove to be more of a challenge than expected, if your understanding of this organ is inaccurate.

Let's get to the heart of the matter

It is "common Knowledge" that the heart is responsible for pumping blood throughout our bodies. Can this premise of the heart's functionality stand up to scrutiny?

The concept of the heart being a pump was first proposed by Giovanni Alphonso Borelli, a 17th century physicist and mathematician who studied under Galileo, and is known for his work in the field of biomechanics.

His theories were later supported by Leonardo Da Vinci which produced drawings of the left ventricle in his notebooks, erroneously showing uniform thickness of the outer walls of the ventricle, as would be expected from a pressurized cavity, when in actual fact the thickness of the walls vary considerably and is so thin at the apex that it can be easily punctured with the prick of a finger. His drawings however have been used in countless medical and biological texts to illustrate an anatomically incorrect portrait of the heart.

An English physician by the name of William Harvey, called the "father of circulatory physiology", also supported the idea that the heart is a pump through his experiments with animals and blood circulation, and published his theories in 1628, which opened the door for others such as Stephen Hales, Jean-Leonard-Marie Poiseuille and Scipione Riva-Rocci to expand upon this theory, leading to our modern understanding of cardiovascular physiology.

René Descartes however, who did agree with Harvey's analyses of blood circulation, did not believe that the circulation was created through the involuntary muscle contractions of the heart acting as pump, but rather compared the heart to a furnace which heats the blood, and as it expands, is forced out into the vascular system where it cools off again as it flows through the veins.

Although our modern academic foundations have come to accept this model of the heart being a pump, there are still many problems with this theory that have yet to be addressed.

There is an old saying which still holds true today… Fluid dynamics is divided into hydraulic engineers that can observe what can't be explained, and mathematicians who can explain what can't be observed.

We can start to understand the problems associated with this concept when we consider that the heart has to pump approximately eight thousand liters of blood every day, non-stop, through a staggering sixty-thousand miles of blood vessels.

In other words, if you were to line up all of the blood vessels of an adult human end to end, it would encircle the earth almost three times, and the heart has to pump a fluid that is five times thicker than water, through these tens of thousands of miles of blood vessels, and through capillaries that often have diameters smaller than red blood cells themselves.

It is estimated that the amount of pressure needed to move this amount of blood is about ten thousand times the amount of pressure that can be generated by the heart.

The circulation of blood in this manner becomes even more perplexing when you consider that in order to facilitate the exchange of nutrients and waste, the blood actually stops moving through the capillaries and oscillates back and forth before continuing its journey back to the heart.

Various observations and measurements of the pressure and velocity of blood through the heart, are not consistent with certain fundamental characteristics of mechanical pumps.

In an interview with Mike Mutzel on his YouTube channel called High Intensity Health, Dr. Thomas Cowan, a Medical Doctor and author of "Human Heart, Cosmic Heart", explains that blood exits the heart at the same velocity as it enters the heart, which should not be the case in a pressure propulsion system. When the blood is pumped out of the left ventricle, the pressure should cause the aortic arch to straighten out, yet the opposite occurs, indicating that the aorta is experiencing a negative pressure.[33]

Imagine attaching a garden hose to a spigot and creating a U-shaped curve in the hose. When the valve is opened and the water pressure comes rushing in, the hose will naturally want to straighten out from the pressure, yet the opposite is true when observing the aortic arch.

He goes on to describe the flow problem through the capillaries, by comparing it with a garden hose that is attached to a spigot with pressurized water that is run down a hill into a stagnant pond, upon which the water must make it back up the hill through another hose. Getting the water to flow back up the hill through this second hose would require the use of a separate pump at the pond, to pump the water back up the hill. The pressure being used to pump the water to the pond cannot force the water back through the second hose and up the hill. How then does the heart keep pumping the blood after it has come to a complete stop inside the capillaries?

In an experiment conducted at St Bartholomew's Hospital Medical College to measure the velocity of blood flow in the rabbit aorta, it shows the velocity peaking before the pressure, when in fact, a liquid at rest will exert an initial resistance to the pressure before moving, and should indicate a peak pressure before a peak in velocity.[34] (p. 336, 337)

It may be prudent to question this concept of the heart being a mechanical pump when we consider these anomalies, and the fact that the physiological composition of the heart is not robust enough to sustain the amount of pressure needed to pump the blood throughout the body.

How then is the blood circulated through the body?

According to Ralph Marinelli et al, authors of "The Heart is not a Pump: A Refutation of the Pressure Propulsion Premise of Heart Function", in 1932, Dr. John Lewis Bremer, an embryologist and professor of anatomy at Harvard University, had documented the blood of the early embryo already circulating in self-propelled spiraling motions before the heart had even developed.[35]

We can therefore deduce that the heart is not a pressure pump, and the blood is propelled by its own momentum. The heart and arteries serve to boost the spiraling motions of the blood.

The spiral shape, or vortex is a fundamental geometric structure of life and is found everywhere in nature such as in pine-cones, sea shells, the DNA molecule etc., and the heart is no exception. A Spanish cardiologist named Fransisco Torrent-Guasp, known as "the man who unfolded a thousand hearts", discovered that the heart was in fact a single muscular band, or tube, that is folded onto itself in a sixty-degree helical formation, and can be described as a type of vortex machine.

Viktor Schauberger, an Austrian scientist and inventor who was fascinated with natural water flows and vortices, and incorporated the vortex in many of his designs such as the Trout Turbine, discovered that flowing water will create vortices along its path and will actually reshape the molecular structure of the water into organized geometric patterns. This structured water is also found throughout the cells in our bodies.

Dr. Gerald Pollack is a biomedical engineer who discovered a fourth phase of water between liquid and solid. This plasma like state of water, often labelled as gel water, structured water, or exclusion zone water, has an extra hydrogen molecule, as well as an extra oxygen molecule (H_3O_2), making it thicker than H_2O. – https://www.pollacklab.org/

Experiments conducted at the Pollack laboratory centers have documented that when water comes in contact with a hydrophilic surface… meaning a surface that attracts water… it will naturally form a layer of gel water next to the surface, where diverse solutes are excluded.

Utilizing a tube made of nafion… a hydrophilic substance… it was discovered that along the inner surface of the tube is an exclusion zone where water exists in a gel-like state (H_3O_2), and little to no soluble materials can be seen, while the normal water (H_2O) that contains dissolved substances naturally flows in the central plane of the tube alongside this exclusion zone.

It was also discovered that this fourth phase of water is negatively charged, and will grow in size when exposed to an energy source such as UV light, visible and near infra-red wavelengths, and also the energy of the earth and human touch. The water that flows alongside is oppositely charged, therefore creating a battery that can produce current.

The walls of our blood vessels, capillaries and arteries are very similar to the nafion tubes and their hydrophilic inner walls become lined with structured water. As approximately 51% of our blood is water, this negatively charged exclusion zone continuously propels the positively charged water/blood through the blood vessels, and will continue to do so indefinitely, provided there is sufficient energy available to allow the water to separate the charges.

According to Dr. Cowan, when the blood enters the heart through the cavity of the left ventricle, a valve momentarily stops the blood from flowing, and as the blood keeps flowing in, it creates a positive pressure that expands the walls on the positive side and creates a negative pressure on the other side of the valve that creates a vacuum and contracts the aortic arch. The heart then converts the laminar flow into a vortex and opens the valve to let the blood flow through in a spiraling motion.[33]

The heart therefore, expands and contracts passively due to the movement of the blood, rather than from its own mechanical muscular activity forcibly pushing the blood through.

Blood circulation and heart function can therefore be described in the following manner:

The heart's main function is to create vortices which structures the water molecules in the blood and accelerates the spiraling movement of the blood. When the water comes in contact with the hydrophilic surface of the inner tubes of blood vessels and capillaries, it creates a thin, gel-like exclusion zone of water.

Charged by various sources of energy, the exclusion zone becomes negatively charged, while the bulk water flowing inside the blood vessels remains positively charged, therefore creating a natural propulsion effect that circulates the blood throughout the blood vessels, arteries and capillaries, and propels itself back to the heart where it enters the left ventricle to resume the process.

The same phenomenon is used to create the flow of water inside plants. The xylem tubes that carry water throughout plants and trees are lined with a hydrophilic protein, creating a negatively charged exclusion zone that separates the charge and forces the positive ions that are centered inside the tube, up the trunks and stems of plants, in much the same way that blood is propelled through our veins.

The natural construct of this realm is so wonderfully designed and self-sustaining. Perhaps our scientists could develop a better understanding of our world and biological systems, by releasing their biases, and opening their minds to alternative concepts., instead of running around in circles trying to prove their erroneous theories.

Is it not sensible to assume a correlation between the leading cause of death in men and women around the world today, i.e. heart disease, and the fact that our medical establishments have adopted a completely erroneous model of our circulatory system and of the heart's functionality?

Scientists have been struggling for decades trying to build a reliable artificial heart. Imagine the breakthroughs in this field if they were to recognize and adopt this new model of blood circulation, instead of trying to replace a passive organ like the heart with a machine that tries to mechanically pump blood through the veins of the trusting patient.

Truth is that our medical system has been designed to hide the real causes of most illnesses afflicting so many people in today's modern world, and in order to understand the reasons for this massive subversion of our scientific and medical institutions, we must also reveal the source of this grand scheme, and their reasons for corrupting the truth.

It is here that we discover the true meaning of the old adage, "All roads lead to Rome."

Chapter 8

THE HEAD OF THE SNAKE

"Some of the biggest men in the United States, in the field of commerce and manufacture, are afraid of something. They know that there is a power somewhere so organized, so subtle, so watchful, so interlocked, so complete, so pervasive, that they had better not speak above their breath when they speak in condemnation of it."[36] – *Woodrow Wilson – 28th President of the United States*

"But there is a very dangerous religious society which would have never been admitted on the soil of the Empire, the Society of Jesus. Its doctrines are subversive of all monarchical principles. The General of the Jesuits desires to be sovereign master, the sovereign of sovereigns. Everywhere that the Jesuits are admitted, they strive for power, at any price. Their society is domineering by nature, and therefore an enemy, and an irreconcilable enemy of all existing powers. Any action, any crime, however atrocious it may be, is a meritorious act, if committed in the interest of the society, or by the orders of its General."[37] (p. 294-295) – *Napoleon Bonaparte (unofficial translation by this author)*

"The organization of the [Roman Catholic] Hierarchy is a complete military despotism, of which the Pope is the ostensible head; but of which, the Black Pope is the real head. The Black Pope is the head of the order of the Jesuits, and is called a General. He not only has command of his own order, but directs and controls the general policy of the Church. He is the power behind the throne, and is the real potential head of the Hierarchy. The whole machine is under the strictest rules of military discipline. The whole thought and will of this machine, to plan, propose and execute, is found in its head. There is no independence of thought, or of action, in its subordinate parts. Implicit and unquestioning obedience to the orders of superiors in authority, is the sworn duty of the priesthood of every grade…"[38] [(p.48)] — *Brigadier General Thomas M. Harris*

Star Trek fans might be disillusioned to discover that Captain Kirk of the Enterprise is actually an allusion to this Jesuit/Catholic conspiracy. The word "kirk" stems from the Scottish word "church", alluding to the fact that the "church" is "captain" of the "enterprise".

This is an organized, secretive army of soldiers, infiltrated in our schools and universities, churches and charity organizations, governments and banking institutions, with the sole purpose of serving their order, in a plot for complete world dominance.

Throughout history, they have been expelled from approximately one hundred countries around the world for various reasons such as political subversion, infiltration, and inciting insurrection, but always return with renewed determination.

They control the international banking systems, most governments around the world, the C.F.R., the Illuminati, the Club of Rome, Opus Dei, the Masons, the New Age Movement, and are the largest land owners in the world.

They rule over the largest Christian church in the world i.e., the Catholic Church, and Pope Francis is the first Jesuit to have been elected as Pope.

They were instrumental in the foundation of America and Canada during the colonization period, which is further substantiated by the fact that there is a Catholic church in almost every small town and city across North America, and many more around the world. They operated churches, nunneries, orphanages, schools, hospitals and insane asylums, and held great influence amongst the settlers.

Back in the 1950's, growing up in a small catholic community in Manitoba, my parents recall having to put on their Sunday best when the Jesuit priest would come to visit. The priests were held in such high regard that the people in the parishes did not question their intentions as they took inventory of their possessions to determine the amount of donations that they were capable of giving to the church for that particular year. People were asked to disclose their net worth, including tractors, horses, farm animals, size of acreage, and if they were planning on expanding their operation in the near future. They would also take inventory of the children, and asked if they were expecting, or planning on growing their family.

During these times, virtually every small town had a catholic church, and most had a presbytery and a nun's convent. They were imbedded in our schooling system and it was not uncommon to have nuns as teachers. I was myself taught by nuns in several elementary school classes, and this practice continued up until the early 1980's.

Today, they control our educational systems, our health care systems, our entertainment industries and the media.

They are accomplished mathematicians, physicists, geologists, map-makers, engineers and astronomers.

Although we have been led to believe that there have always been ideological rivalries between religious beliefs and what we now call "science", curiously, the church was in fact the architect of our modern scientific doctrines.

Author Thomas Woods refutes the age-old prejudice that the church's superstitions and position was an impediment to scientific and technological progress, and instead points to the church as being the primary influence on the modernization of our Western civilization, introducing an extensive body of knowledge and understanding of our physical universe.[39,40]

Jonothan Wright states in his book that the Jesuits were instrumental in the development of telescopes, microscopes, clocks, barometers, electricity and astronomy, as well as theories on the circulation of blood and the wave-like nature of light.[41]

According to the Jesuits themselves, in 1750, 30 of the world's 130 astronomical observatories were managed by Jesuit astronomers, and approximately 35 lunar craters have been named in honor of Jesuit scientists.

The following is a list of a few of the innumerable Jesuits who have contributed to the development of our modern-day scientific knowledge.

Christoph Clavius – Jesuit astronomer who helped create the Gregorian calendar

Father Giambattista Riccioli – Experimented with pendulums, and is the first person to measure the rate of acceleration of free-falling bodies

Jean-Félix Picard – French astronomer that was honored with a pyramid at Juvisy-sur-Orge for being the first person to accurately measure the size of the earth

Father Georges Lemaitre – Theoretical physicist, mathematician and astronomer who invented the Big Bang Theory

Dr. George Gheverghese Joseph – Identified the basic components of calculus called the "infinite series", wrongly attributed to Sir Isaac Newton and Gottfried Leibnitz.

Father J.B. Macelwane – Wrote the first seismology textbook in America in 1936

Father Athanasius Kircher – Father of Germ Theory, father of Egyptology

Father Roger Boscovich – Father of modern atomic theory

The Jesuits were also responsible for introducing western science and mathematics to various countries such as China, and were well-known for their knowledge of astronomy, mathematics, geography and hydraulics

Considering the Jesuit's vast influence, is it possible that they could have purposefully subverted our sciences? What would be the purpose of orchestrating such a deception?

If humanity can be coerced into believing in a false model of reality where virtually everything in our lives have been corrupted or falsified, the mind can be so completely absorbed in this fake reality, that it is incapable of forming any kind of opposition to a system it cannot even begin to comprehend.

An organization that controls information, can control the world. Therefore, it is only logical to assume that the Jesuits could have purposely confiscated our knowledge base with the aspirations of replacing it with false doctrines meant to subdue humanity to their will.

If the greatest of our technological marvels have been confiscated and concealed from the general public, such innovations could be used against an ignorant populace for nefarious purposes.

They might have created astronomical, scientific and space organizations worldwide… and convinced us that we landed on the moon… in an attempt to cure our reluctance to believe in space and space exploration, which can then be used to convince people of the existence of extraterrestrial life, which can be used to distract the public with fantastic stories of space and government cover-ups, and to indoctrinate and prepare the populace for a planned fake alien invasion that will be used to unite the world under a single governing body.

This scenario was openly discussed by America's 40th president, Ronald Reagan, at a speech before the United Nations in 1987.

"Perhaps we need some outside universal threat to make us recognize this common bond. I occasionally think how quickly our differences worldwide would vanish if we were facing an alien threat from outside this world."[42]

Reagan showed great interest in the National Aeronautics and Space Administration, launching the Space Shuttle program, and initiating the development of a manned space station. He also approved an ambitious new space policy aimed at developing a lunar base and manned flights to Mars.

Does anyone still believe we actually landed on the moon?

It is alleged, that using 1960's technology, we strapped 3 men into a can sitting on top of a large rocket, shot them out of the atmosphere into a vacuum where they flew across the emptiness of space, (surviving the deadly Van Allen radiation belt), all the way to the moon, attained orbit, climbed aboard a lunar lander and shot down to the surface of the moon, then embarked on a Lunar Roving Vehicle deployed from the lander, drove around on the surface of the moon and played golf, hopped back into the lunar lander, rocketed off the moon, and successfully docked back with the orbiting vehicle travelling at thousands of miles per hour, and rocketed back to earth, where they burned through the atmosphere and landed in the ocean where they were recovered.

A quick note on vacuums; Even our best vacuum chambers on earth cannot reproduce the claimed vacuum of space.

The largest vacuum chamber on earth is the Space Power Facility in Sandusky Ohio. The walls are constructed of a sealed steel membrane, 1/4" thick, sandwiched between 6 feet of concrete.

The space suits worn by astronauts consist of 11 layers of material with a total thickness of 3/16", while the shield on their helmets is 1/5" thick... and this we are told, protects the astronauts from a vacuum which is significantly less dense than the best vacuum achievable on earth.

Of course, NASA could easily put an end to the skepticism surrounding the moon landings by providing the data accumulated during the missions, but unfortunately, as confirmed by astronaut Don Pettit,[43] we are told that they have "destroyed" all of the data.

Richard Nafzger, an engineer at NASA's Goddard Space Flight Center in Maryland further substantiated this claim, stating that the tapes were part of a batch of approximately two-hundred thousand that were magnetically erased to save money.[44]

You would think that the details associated with the most impressive achievement ever attributed to humankind would be important enough to merit safe keeping.

Funny to note that the moon rock given to the Dutch Prime Minister by the Apollo 11 astronauts after their mission was examined by a group of Dutch scientists, and turned out to be a piece of petrified wood.

Did NASA fake the moon landings? Do we have any reason to doubt NASA's authenticity? Could the sole existence of this space agency be attributed to mass deception?

Enter Operation Paperclip…

Operation Paperclip was a secret program created after the second world war to recruit and relocate to the United States., ex-Nazi scientists and engineers, to help create and establish the new space program. NASA was formed by German,

WWII, Nazi scientists such as Wernher Von Braun and others who worked on the V-2 rocket for the third Reich.

Is it truly wise to put our trust in an organization that was formed using members of the German Nazi Party, whose leader was trained by the Jesuits?

Can we not consider that the same organization (the Jesuits), which has led countless millions to their death in wars and conflicts, having convinced them of performing atrocious acts against humanity in the name of religious dogma or illusory threats to their wellbeing, might have the audacity to skew our concept of the reality in which we exist?

Do you believe that today's scientifically advanced society has surpassed such tactics of indoctrination?

Do you believe that you, personally could not be manipulated to act in certain ways that are destructive to yourself and others?

Do you believe that your current understanding of the world is a proven fact that cannot be questioned?

Do you believe that your government's current use of military resources is justified?

Do you believe that your government could not possibly be lying to the public they serve and are acting out of a general concern for your safety and security?

If so, then I should wish to welcome you to the world of mind control.

We have been trained to believe that we live in a free and open society and must protect ourselves from terrorists and religious fanatics who wish to destroy our peaceful way of life, and will reject any notion that the same brainwashing techniques that are utilized on others, could also be applied to manipulate our way of thinking.

We will sit by and watch as our governments strip us of our rights and freedoms, force us to acquiesce to mask mandates and personal health violations, attack and incarcerate any who choose to exercise their rights, make use of our police and military forces to quell all opposition to their directives, and suppress any who threaten their authority.

When we honestly examine the degree to which we are already manipulated, should we not consider the extent to which this influence could be used today?

Should we not consider the possibility that our sciences could be a part of this indoctrination?

Should we not consider that a global organization such as the Jesuits could have undermined our most trusted institutions?

They also provide an education to over 2.5 million students, through 3,730 Jesuit schools that they have established worldwide, including over 200 institutions of higher learning.

Their graduates have established themselves throughout the world as politicians, lawyers, judges, television producers, famous actors, sports celebrities, musicians, film directors, writers, journalists, mathematicians, physicists, astronomers, architects, billionaire investors and business owners, university professors, bankers, CEO's and more.

There are countless literary works describing the vast influence of this organization in all aspects of our lives and their despotic agendas and ruthless determination to achieve their goals. However, I believe we can safely conclude that this Order of the Jesuits most assuredly has the means and conviction to drastically alter our perceptions of this world, and crucial to this reformation, is the re-writing of our history books.

Chapter 9
OUR HIDDEN HISTORY

A recently declassified CIA document from 1957 has sparked an unprecedented worldwide interest concerning our seemingly fabricated history. It outlines the Russian eradication of the ancient empire of Tartary and its subsequent deletion from our history books.

Many old maps depict a large country named Tartaria, covering an area of over three million square miles, located in the Asian continent.

The following is an excerpt from page 10 of the document titled "National Cultural Development Under Communism", written in June of 1957.

"Or let us take the matter of history, which, along with religion, language and literature, constitute the core of a people's cultural heritage. Here again the Communists have interfered in a shameless manner. For example, on 9 August 1944, the Central committee of the Communist Party, sitting in Moscow, issued directive ordering the party's Tartar Provincial Committee "to proceed to a scientific revision of the history of Tartaria, to liquidate serious shortcomings and mistakes of a nationalistic character committed by individual writers and historians in dealing with Tartar history." In other words, Tartar history was to be rewritten – let us be frank, was to be falsified – in order to eliminate references to Great Russian aggressions and to hide the facts of the real course of Tartar-Russian relations. And this was no isolated case. In every

Muslim area within the USSR, historians, on orders of the Communist Party, have rewritten history to distort the facts so that the Russians appear always in a good light. Needless to say, histories which present the facts truthfully have been withdrawn and destroyed, so that the present and future generations of Muslims are forever denied the chance of learning the true facts of their nations' past."[45] (p. 9)

This document was written during the cold war between Russia and the United States of America, and was no doubt part of the U.S. administration's efforts to ensure needed Muslim support, by showcasing Russia's disgraceful treatment of various cultures under communist rule.

The United States Information Agency targeted the Saudis with propaganda campaigns denouncing the oppressive and violent treatment of Muslims in communist countries, in contrast with the religious tolerances of the United States.[46]

Regardless of its contextual pretense, the revelations of historical manipulations outlined in the CIA document are an important aspect to consider, as it is further evidence that history is often re-written by those in power to suit their narratives.

Many have now come to believe that the Tatarians were an advanced society teeming with technological marvels, and that their power and influence spread throughout the world, evidenced by common architectural designs and construction methods.

However, such as is common today, technological advances may be shared throughout various cultures around the world without ascribing its unique tenure to one individual culture.

The CIA document not only mentions the falsification of Tartarian history, but also of various other Muslim cultures. It would therefore be imprudent to attribute the architectural and technological advances commonly seen in all parts of the world as stemming from one particular culture, as the falsification of history was not uniquely directed towards Tartaria.

No one can be certain of what exactly transpired in the past, but upon closer examination of available data, there can be no doubt that most of our historical timeline has been fabricated.

The enormous buildings and astounding architecture found worldwide reveals a narrative which in no way correlates to the given timelines of their construction, with respect to the technologies we are told were available at their time of construction.

Furthermore, a strange anomaly persists throughout the world, where buildings and infrastructure seem to have been partially buried in sand or dirt. This phenomenon points to a worldwide event or cataclysm which presumably wiped out a significant portion of the population of this world, and in some instances, completely buried entire cities.

You need only take a look at many of the older buildings in most cities around the world, and notice that the bottom windows of the structures are partially submerged in the earth, buried in plain sight.

It would seem that most of the cities in North America and many other countries around the world are much older than presumed, and were constructed by an advanced civilization that, along with their knowledge, was written out of existence.

Today's churches, cathedrals, temples, arches, domes, and colosseums were re-purposed to suit a different narrative, and hide their true origin.

I took on the arduous task of cataloging as many of the buildings erected in the city of Winnipeg in Manitoba, between the time when the first settlers arrived in the 18th century, and 1920. The purpose being, to examine their time of construction, length of time to build, materials used, construction methods, tools and technology available, as well as the mining, manufacturing and transportation of building materials and tools necessary for their construction, in order to determine the feasibility of building such structures, with respect to the conditions and populations in the era in which they were built.

Although this project is a work in progress that will be made available to the public upon its completion, I would like to share some of the data I've accumulated, to shed some light on our present historical narrative.

The establishment of the city of Winnipeg began with the arrival of a French explorer by the name of Pierre Gaultier de Varennes, sieur de La Verendrye, in 1738.

By 1869, a few forts had been constructed in the area, and no fewer than thirty houses and commercial structures were grouped around the intersection of Portage and Main, accommodating an estimated population of 215.

In 1870, with a population of 300, Winnipeg consisted of thirty, mostly temporary structures, including the Ritchot Orphanage, and it was noted by Sir Adam Archibald, the first Lieutenant Governor of Manitoba, that when he first reached

Winnipeg in 1870, there were five post offices and three mail routes.

The population grew to approximately 700 by 1871, at which time the Manitoba College and the Market Building were constructed. By 1874, the population had grown to approximately 5000 residents, and the total number of buildings was estimated at over 900, including dwellings, saloons, manufacturing buildings, banks, butcher shops, book stores, tailors, fur stores, drug stores etc., and over 400 miscellaneous buildings.[47]

Extrapolating from this historical narrative, let us point out certain anomalies.

Why did 300 colonists, living in a small town consisting of thirty houses and commercial structures in 1870, need five post offices? Shouldn't one post office have been sufficient?

Why would a group of seven hundred settlers that are struggling to survive Manitoba's harsh climate, living in temporary structures, having rudimentary tools with a transportation system consisting of horses and carts, need to build a large, architecturally impressive college, with materials which were not readily available at the time, for a handful of students? *(Pictures of this college and of Winnipeg at the time is available in the "Old World" section of my website – pendulumsofpower.com)*

All available man-power at the time would have surely been needed to help in basic survival needs. How many families at the time would have sacrificed their most productive workers to send them to college?

Growing up in a small town in Manitoba, I can attest to the fact that even as recently as the 1980's, certain children were still pulled out of school to go work on the family farm.

We could estimate the number of children at the time to have been approximately 200-250. Spreading out the age differential, there may have been 5 to 20 children per classroom. Assuming all children were attending school on a regular basis, managed to pass their courses, graduate, and also decided to pursue post-secondary education, the best-case scenario is that maybe 1 to 5 graduates might have attended college. Shouldn't an easy to build wooden structure have been sufficient for such needs? We can of course assume that graduates from across the province may have attended the college, but again, who would sacrifice their fittest workers?

According to the University of Winnipeg records, the Manitoba College was founded in 1871, and taught its first class on November 10th, 1871, to a total of seventeen students. The records however indicate that they were situated in another location called Nisbet Hall.[48]

In a section called "Manitoba College in Pictures" on the U of W website, there is a picture of the Manitoba College and the caption reads that it first opened in October of 1882. The records are not clear regarding students that were taught in this building, but its construction is stated to have been completed in 1871, according to multiple sources.[48]

Already faced with difficulties obtaining basic supplies, how were the colonists in 1871 able to gain access to the materials necessary to build an impressive brick structure.

Furthermore, brick manufacturing in this area at the time of its construction was virtually non-existent. Even the bricks being manufactured in 1873 were of poor quality.

According to David Butterfield, in his book "A History of Brick Manufacturing in Manitoba, 1860-1990", A man named John Christian Schultz had started a brick-yard in 1868, and had apparently completed the first brick building to be erected in Winnipeg in October of 1868. However, the bricks were apparently malformed and unusable.[49] (p. 34-35)

There were no rail lines to this area in 1871, and the thought of using the horse drawn Red River cart, or waste valuable steam boat transportation to haul tens of thousands of bricks to build a massive college for a small group of settlers in the backwoods of Manitoba is absurd.

In the "Old World" section of my website, I have posted photographs and drawings of the Portage and Main area of Winnipeg, illustrating what the city looked like from 1869 to 1872.

Extrapolating from these images, we could safely deduce that the town had not grown in any significant way, as the images are fairly similar, and in some cases virtually identical.

The observations of Winnipeg in 1872 by W. J. Healy describes a small town consisting of a few randomly dispersed shacks.[50]

However, there is a map that was published in the Manitoba Free Press in 1922 that outlines the locations of over 70 buildings around the Portage and Main area of Winnipeg in 1872.

The caption for the map substantiates its authenticity through careful verification by people who lived in Winnipeg at the time. Although the caption dates the map as 1873, the map itself is dated as 1872.

"The above chart shows the location of the buildings public and private, in the village of Winnipeg proper (the center of which was then as it is now, the corner of Main and Portage roads) in 1873. Two noted buildings adjoining the village, to the north – but not in the village – do not appear in the chart and should be mentioned here. These were Manitoba college and the first Winnipeg public school, which stood not far from the present site of the C.P.R. buildings. The buildings shown have been carefully checked and their positions verified by old-time residents of Winnipeg."[51]

Once again, we are left with contradictory historical records, and must therefore hypothesize that either a) The Manitoba Free Press records have been wrongly dated, b) The photographs and images are wrongly dated, c) The photographs and images are not of Winnipeg and have been mistakenly labelled as Winnipeg, or d) Our historical records have been fabricated to record a counterfeit historical narrative, and conceal the real history of the old world.

Examining the Manitoba College, you will also notice that the bottom windows are partially built underground. Which also meant the excavation of hundreds of yards of soil with rudimentary shovels. Furthermore, after suffering massive flooding in the area about once a decade, why would any sane person decide that it would be a good idea to build windows that extend into the ground?

If Winnipeg did indeed consist of a few shacks in 1872, and the photographs and drawings are indeed an accurate depiction of the area at the time, then it would seem that Winnipeg grew from a small town consisting of approximately thirty mostly temporary structures, to over nine hundred buildings… not to mention over 4,000 yards of sidewalks and over 400 miscellaneous structures, in the span of just two years.

We must consider the fact that there were no power tools, front end loaders, cranes, trucks, excavators, paved roads or rail lines available at the time. Trees would have to be manually cut down and hauled to the saw mills by horse power. What building methods were used to construct so many structures?

We must also consider the limitations set by the climate of this area, as the harsh winters do not permit the construction of certain types of buildings during that season. Excavation would have been virtually impossible, and certainly not considered. Brick and mortar construction can only be accomplished in the summer months. Although wooden structures can be erected during the winter, most of the construction endeavors would have been contained within the six-month period spanning from May to November.

Many of the structures built around this time, and up until the early 1900's, are recorded as being built in impossible timeframes and unrealistic start times which span the construction process throughout the winter months.

For example: The Isbister school is a three-story brick building, with a tower extending to five stories high, and is the oldest standing school in Winnipeg. Construction is said to have begun in the third week of June 1898, with the official corner stone laying ceremony taking place on September 26th, and officially opened on March 27, 1899.

The interior of the building had spacious well-lit classrooms, oak staircases with finely carved and varnished wooden banisters, stained-glass windows, wainscotting and much more.

Examining the historical weather records for Winnipeg during the time of its construction we find that it was an exceptionally cold winter, with nightly lows exceeding -30 degrees Celsius forty-one times from December to March, with ten days exceeding -40 degrees Celsius.

The construction timeline of just over nine months, given for the erection of this building, considering excavation, foundation work, exterior construction and finishing, interior construction and finishing, size and complexity of the structure and the weather at the time of its construction, is unrealistic, even for today's standards.

Browsing through archives, you will notice that in most instances, we are not given timelines for the construction of buildings, and instead, are only told that it was built in a particular year. We have to assume therefore that most buildings were built within the span of one year or less.

It would seem that the people at the time were masters of construction and could magically throw up buildings in record times, especially after the arrival of the first transport trains, which permitted materials to be more readily available.

The Canadian Pacific Railway (CPR) arrived in Winnipeg in July of 1881, and after a decade of apparently suppressed energy, the city began to throw up an assortment of buildings which were, for some odd reason, apparently just as quickly demolished and re-built.[52] (p. 5)

Are we to accept that this is our true historical narrative? That the settlers in the late 1800's were so incredibly adept at construction that they would just "throw up" a wild assortment of buildings, teeming with details inside and out, and once done, they would step back and look at them and think to themselves… "I don't really like this one… lets tear it down and build another one in its place".

Are we to consider that many of the architects looking for opportunities in the new world were just terrible at designing new buildings, and that no one was keen enough to notice the design flaws or unpleasant aesthetics, until after the buildings were fully constructed?

Are we to assume that the settlers didn't have the common sense to approve the look and design of a building at the blueprint stage of the process, rather than changing their minds after the building had been constructed?

In the decade preceding the arrival of the train, the town grew from a population of a few hundred settlers to about twenty thousand, and during this time, the inhabitants built over a thousand structures, including dwellings, businesses, manufacturing plants, stables, government buildings, universities and colleges, schools, churches, banks, hotels and bridges. They brought in electric lights, the telegram, street cars, built miles of roads and sidewalks, and laid 100 kilometers of track to accommodate a thirty-two-thousand-pound steam locomotive… which was said to have been transported to Winnipeg by barge on the river… and after a decade of staggering achievements, they still had pent up energy? I can see this being relevant if they had spent the last ten years sitting around whittling sticks on their porch, but their accomplishments were nothing less than extraordinary.

Their pent up energy did continue to serve them well as they persisted in building more colleges and universities, schools, residential blocks, luxurious hotels, churches, bridges, theaters, hospitals, orphanages, businesses, government buildings, amusement parks with automatic swings, a shooting gallery, a moving picture or "kinetoscope" tent, a bandstand, a merry-go round, an 800 person dance pavilion, bumper cars, carousels, a massive roller coaster, Ferris wheel, harness racing track, dance hall, roller rink, zoo, miniature train, sports facilities for tennis and softball, and in the winter, ice skating and ski jumping… and by 1904 had completed 17 miles of asphalt, 33 miles of macadam, 16 miles of block pavement, 23 miles of artificial stone, 186 miles of plank walks, 99 miles of water mains, 87 miles of sewers and 65 miles of boulevard throughout the city.

According to David Butterfield, many of the brick buildings being built in Manitoba at the time would have required approximately one million bricks respectively, and considering the thousands of comparable structures being built across the prairies, it would suggest a demand for billions of bricks.[49] (p. 2)

The materials needed to construct so many buildings is astounding when you consider that beyond just the billions of bricks that needed to be manufactured, there was also a need for mortar, trowels, shovels, hand saws, hammers, wheelbarrows, ladders, scaffolding, carts, horses, saddles, rope, chains, paint, brushes, hardware, architectural finishings, marble, staircases and railings, doors, hinges, door knobs, locks, windows, wallpaper, plumbing, pumps, toilets, sinks, bathtubs, faucets, electrical wires, light fixtures, light bulbs, wood stoves, radiators… and adding to that, the materials used in everyday life, including chairs, tables, cooking stoves, pots, pans, utensils, bottles, jars, cups, plates, bowls, beds, materials for bedding and clothing, needles and thread, boots, shoes, laces, hats, desks, pens, ink, paper products, books, clocks, lamps, oil, firewood, toys, scissors, hair brushes, shaving cream, mirrors, mops, pails, soap, barrels, guns and rifles, holsters, ammunition, gun powder, traps, snowshoes, tobacco, whiskey, sugar, flour and food products of all kinds, gardening tools, harvesting tools, blacksmithing tools, axes, photographic cameras… not to mention the materials needed to build roads, sidewalks, bridges, pontoon bridges, rail lines, street cars, water mains, sewer systems, mining equipment, amusement parks, steam engines, saw mills, planers and a host of other materials and tools needed for a variety of manufactured products.

Many of these products were apparently already in use before the first train even arrived in Winnipeg.

Construction of the first railway to be built in Manitoba began on the 29th of September, 1877, and its completion is commemorated on a plaque in Dominion City, which reads.

"On December 3, 1878, the last spike was driven here to complete the first railway line built in the Canadian West. Known as the Pembina Branch, it ran some 100 kilometers from St. Boniface to the international boundary at Emerson." – https://www.readtheplaque.com/plaque/first-railway-in-western-canada

As the first spikes were driven at the onset of winter, how was the landscaping and laying of the ballast bed over a distance of 100 kilometers accomplished throughout the winter months?

The construction of this rail line would have required approximately 180,000 rail ties, which would have required the cutting down and hauling of approximately 1,000 trees every week to the sawmills, which would then have to produce an average of 2,763 rail ties every single week, or 396 ties/day, to then be treated and hauled to the rail line for transport to its final position. This would also be over and above the incredible amount of lumber which needed to be produced to keep up with the unsatiable appetite for the construction of buildings and other structures in the area at the time.

It would have also required approximately 21,868 thirty-foot rails, 360,000 spikes, 21,866 perforated metal plates, and tens of thousands of bolts.

Assuming they were able to work 24 hours/day, every day during its construction, they would have had to been able to consistently install 720 feet of track every day. Which meant installing 396 rail ties and 48 rails every day, or one rail tie every 4 minutes, and one rail every 30 minutes.

If they were indeed able to build 720 feet of track every day, why is it that four years after its completion, in 1882, the Winnipeg Street Railway was incorporated and they stipulated that one mile of track must be laid within six months? Shouldn't they have been able to build a mile of track in just a few days?

It's important to remember that these numbers were calculated based on consistent, non-stop 24 hours/day, un-interrupted, problem free operation in all areas of the construction process. Realistically however, they likely didn't work more than 8-10 hours/day, considering the season in which they were building the railroad. This meant laying one rail tie every 1½ minutes, and one rail every 12 minutes.

Numerous historical accounts of railroad construction in Canada make reference to the "construction season", and to the summer months having longer daylight hours in which to work, casting even more doubt on this endeavor.[53, 54]

These examples were derived from the construction of the CPR railroad across western Canada, which is said to have started in Bonfield, Ontario on February 18th, 1881, and was completed on November 7th, 1885, at a distance of 3454 kilometers to Craigellachie in British Columbia, and was apparently completed six years ahead of schedule.

Considering the harsh terrain and environment in which the workers had to lay track, it is very unlikely that the construction of railroads would have been possible throughout the winter months.

Assuming a work season of 7 months, and an average workday of 15 hours, being able to lay down 3454 km of track throughout 5 seasons would have required the laying of almost 6,000 rail ties/day… or 1 rail tie every 10 seconds, as well as 721 rails/day… or 1 rail every 50 seconds.

Add to this the enormous amount of soil necessary to make paths through swamplands that are rigid enough to support the immense weight of the trains, as well as the bridges and massive trestles that needed to be built to get across rivers, canyons and valleys, and having to dynamite through rock to get across the Canadian Shield and to make mountain paths.[55]

Through the prairies, they were apparently able to build 10 km of track/day, which would have required the crews to lay down 18,000 rail ties/day… or 1 rail tie every 3 seconds, and 2,186 rails/day… or 1 rail every 24 seconds.

The logistical implications of such an endeavor might seem unrealistic, yet there are videos on the internet of large organized crews of men laying tracks at an impressive rate in the early 1900's. Therefore, it may be possible to lay track in a very efficient manner, yet, once again, we must remember that all the materials necessary would have to be manufactured and delivered to the site consistently, every day without interruptions in the supply line. How were they able to manufacture thousands of rails every day to keep up with this demand? How were they able to transport 18,000 rails to the site every single day?

We must also account for the construction being periodically delayed for various reasons such as weather conditions or flooding.

Although we may be impressed by the amazing feats accomplished by these settlers on the plains of Manitoba, we may be further astonished by what they were able to achieve beneath the landscape of city streets and buildings.

It is a well-known fact that underneath most of the cities in North America, lay a vast array of subterranean passages, and the city of Winnipeg is no exception.

There are numerous examples of well-known tunnels in the city, including the various underground sections of the Winnipeg Walkway System consisting of 14 skyways and 7 tunnels throughout the downtown area connecting 38 buildings, and an underground mall section called Winnipeg Square, spanning a total of 2km.

Many tunnels were built to accommodate steam pipes and electrical conduits that provided heat and electricity to nearby buildings.

The Eaton's Power House Building was used to provide power and heat to the adjacent T. Eaton & Company store.

A series of 7 foot wide and 10-foot-high underground passages were used to connect the Central Power House to the Manitoba Legislature, Law Courts building and Provincial Archives building amongst others, to provide heating and electrical power to these buildings.

In the Exchange District, the Amy Street Heating Plant provided steam to heat several large buildings throughout the downtown area of Winnipeg, through a labyrinth of underground pipes.[56]

The University of Manitoba, with over one hundred buildings totaling over six million square feet of space, located on a 676-acre piece of land, has a labyrinth of underground corridors connecting several major buildings on campus, and are presently used as walkways, as well as conduits for steam pipes which are utilized to provide heating for several buildings.

There are also tunnels connecting downtown skyscrapers, as well as the Administrative Building and Council Building comprising City Hall, and a tunnel that was dug to run the Greater Winnipeg Water District's aqueduct beneath the bed of the Red River, which we are told had to be filled with concrete to ensure that the water pipe could not move inside the tunnel.

It is presumed that there are several miles of tunnels which are kept secret from the public, and several more which have been either destroyed or made inaccessible. Contractors hired to install and repair plumbing, fire suppression systems, electrical conduits, and more recently, fiber-optic lines, have spoken of the strict security and restrictions imposed in the tunnels. Special clearance is needed to access the tunnels, and movement is restricted to the areas where the work must be performed. Camera equipment is also prohibited.

It was admitted to me by such contractors who have been down in the tunnels several times, that there are untold miles of underground passages reaching several stories deep, and that some are guarded by armed security officers 24/7, and are inaccessible without proper clearance.

The reasoning used by governments to forbid entry to such places is always the same… safety and liability issues. Although I can understand the need to regulate access to such sensitive areas, it does not give them the right to conceal their existence and lie to the public. Naturally, they will hide their treachery using the old plausible deniability routine and just deny their existence, and further support their position through media mind control tactics which discourages further public inquiry.

The seemingly impossible historical narrative attributed to the city of Winnipeg is consistent throughout most of the cities across the entire continent, and if weighed against an alternative history, which reveals a vastly different account of the past and suggests that all of these cities were already built and were merely re-populated by the "settlers" after the worldwide calamity which covered a good part of the earth in mud and soil, we uncover the reasons for the many discrepancies in our timelines and the justifications for all the secrecy surrounding the underground tunnels, as their construction would have been impossible to corroborate with our present historical narrative.

Although some of the old-world infrastructure and technology may have been destroyed by this apocalyptic event, whatever remained that was not to be a part of this new world framework and could not feasibly be removed or destroyed, would have had to been camouflaged behind fabricated historical interpretations.

When examining the 18th and 19th century history of North America, you will notice that at some point during this timeline, virtually every city in North America had suffered a large-scale destruction, either by fire, or by warfare.

I have added the following list to illustrate the staggering number of cities that have had significant fires with large scale destruction during the 17th to the 20th century.

1608 – Jamestown, Virginia – destroyed

1625 – Oslo, Norway – destroyed

1633 – Great Istanbul fire, 20,000 buildings burned

1652 – Glasgow, Scotland, ⅓ of the city destroyed

1657 – Great Fire of Edo, ⅔ of city destroyed, (now Tokyo, Japan)

1660 – Istanbul, Turkey, ⅔ of city destroyed, estimated 40,000 killed

1666 – Great Fire of London, most of city destroyed

1692 – Usingen, Germany, most of city burned

1696 – St. John's Newfoundland, destroyed

1711 – Great Boston fire

1728 – Copenhagen, Denmark, ⅖ of city burned

1734 – Montreal, New France (Canada)

1752 – Moscow, Russia, 18,000 houses destroyed

1760 – Great Boston fire, 349 buildings destroyed

1787 – Great Boston fire, 100 buildings destroyed

1788 – New Orleans fire, 856 of 1,100 buildings burned

1788 – Kyoto, Japan, 37,000 houses burned, 150 deaths

1805 – Detroit, Michigan, destroyed

1811 – Kiev, Russia, 2,000 buildings burned, 30 deaths

1813 – Buffalo, New York, destroyed

1813 – York, Upper Canada

1813 – Portsmouth, New Hampshire, 272 structures burned

1814 – Washington, D.C., destroyed

1816 – St. John's, Newfoundland, 120 structures burned, 1,000 left homeless

1817 – St. John's, Newfoundland

1819 – St. John's Newfoundland, 120 structures burned

1827 – Great fire of Turku, Finland's oldest city, 70% of city burned, 11,000 left homeless

1829 – Augusta, Georgia, 13 separate fires that same year, hundreds of structures burned

1835 – New York City, Second Great Fire

1838 – Charleston, South Carolina, 1,000 buildings destroyed

1845 – New York City, 345 buildings destroyed

1845 – Great Fire of Pittsburgh, 1,000 buildings destroyed

1846 – Great Fire, St. John's, Newfoundland, 2,000 buildings destroyed, 12,000 left homeless

1849 – St. Louis, 3 deaths

1849 – First Great Fire of Toronto, Canada, known as the Cathedral fire

1851 – San Fransisco, 2,000 buildings destroyed

1852 – Great Montreal Fire, 10,000 left homeless

1866 – Great Portland Fire, Maine, 10,000 left homeless

1866 – Great Fire of Quebec City, Quebec, 20,000 left homeless

1871 – Great Chicago Fire, 250 deaths

1872 – Great Boston Fire, 776 buildings destroyed, 20 deaths

1874 – Chicago, 812 buildings destroyed, 20 deaths

1877 – St. John, New Brunswick, 1,600 buildings destroyed

1886 – Calgary, Alberta

1886 – Great Vancouver Fire, British Columbia, 1,000 buildings destroyed

1892 – Great Fire of 1892, St. John's, Newfoundland, destroyed, 12,000 homeless

1894 – Great Fire of Shanghai, China, 1,000 buildings destroyed

1897 – Great Fire of Windsor, Nova Scotia, 80% of town destroyed

1898 – Great Fire of New Westminster, British Columbia

1900 – Hull-Ottawa, Ontario, large part of city destroyed

1900 – Sandon, British Columbia, destroyed

1904 – Second Great Fire of Toronto, Ontario, largest fire in Toronto

1912 – Houston, Texas, 56 city blocks destroyed

1917 – Great Atlanta Fire, 73 city blocks destroyed

These are but a few examples of cities that have suffered large scale fires during this period.

Many wars fought around the world were further responsible for causing massive destruction to innumerable old-world buildings and structures.

The second World War not only claimed the lives of a staggering sixty million souls, but was also responsible for the destruction of millions of buildings throughout Europe and other countries involved in the war. The city of London itself lost over one million buildings.

Allied bombers dropped over 2 million tons of bombs on Germany, destroying 75% of the 54 largest cities with populations greater than 100,000, and over 20% of smaller cities with populations of 25,000 - 100,000, killing over 600,000 people and wiping out almost 5 million housing units.

What is often overlooked and not well known, is the massive carpet bombing of France by the Allied Forces that claimed the lives of 70,000 men, women and children, and leveled 1570 cities and towns across the country.

In the synopsis for his book, Jean-Claude Valla describes the fact that the French people of today remember the atomic bombs dropped on Japan, yet ignore the Anglo-American bombing of their own country that claimed 70,000 lives, noting that the atomic bomb in Hiroshima killed approximately 75,000 people.[57]

I have yet to find a plausible explanation to justify the wanton destruction of French cities by the Allied Forces. Although there can never be any manner of justification for such actions, there were no strategic benefits to these attacks, and as we can see from the quote above, not only have the French people been spared the details of their own history, but it would seem that historical accounts of the war from various countries around the world would rather disregard such uncomfortable truths.

When the Germans invaded the city of Warsaw in Poland, they kept the city under a constant barrage of artillery and air bombing for just over two months, and eventually deported over half a million inhabitants. Once the entire population had been expelled from the city, specialized German combat engineers were sent in to burn and destroy the remaining structures, eradicating 90% of the entire city's buildings, including castles, palaces, historical monuments, theatres, housing units and libraries such as the Zaluski Library, one of the oldest libraries in Europe, and in total, destroyed over sixteen million books, volumes, scrolls, maps and other valuable artifacts preserved in the libraries of Warsaw.

Not only were the Nazis determined to eliminate the cultural heritage of many countries, but the allies also targeted libraries and other structures which stored historical, cultural and technological artifacts in various countries, which together resulted in the eradication and looting of countless volumes and valuable manuscripts, as well as priceless paintings and artworks throughout countries such as Austria, Belarus, Belgium, China, Czechoslovakia, France, Greece, Hungary, Italy, Japan, Latvia, Luxembourg, Malasia, Netherlands, Philippines, the U.K. and more.

Buildings targeted by both sides included cathedrals, churches, medieval structures, palaces, synagogues, castles, historical landmarks, temples and museums, resulting in countless millions of historical treasures being destroyed by the war.

Let's explore the logic of such actions.

The main goal of the Nazi Party was the forced acquisition of the lebensraum, which means "living space". In other words, the expansion of the German territory for the German people.

If you are invading a neighboring country in order to expand living space for your people, wouldn't it be logical to ensure that the infrastructure remains intact, so as to accommodate the new inhabitants?

What is the logic in not only completely leveling entire cities through massive aerial carpet bombing, but continuing a land offensive afterwards to destroy as many of the remaining buildings as possible, even after having conquered the territory and evacuated its inhabitants?

Many of the cities that were destroyed were replete with incredible architecture and beautifully designed buildings, furnished with all the necessities and luxuries of life. Where is the wisdom in obliterating all the roadways, transportation systems, electrical systems, plumbing systems, toilets, bathtubs, cooking equipment, furniture, food etc., if you are to repopulate these cities with your own citizens?

Why were thousands of cities and towns razed to the ground without regard for human life?

We must consider the obvious eradication of the old world, and the history of the peoples who lived in this era, as well as the complete erasure of the most significant of their technological accomplishments.

When browsing through pictures of cities that have been destroyed by carpet bombing, we can also notice the uncanny resemblance to pictures of cities that have been destroyed by fire.

Although some similarities may be expected, realistically, the aftermath of a fire should be noticeably different than that of massive aerial carpet bombing.

In many instances, we are led to believe that the city that burned, mostly consisted of wooden structures that were erected close to one another and facilitated the spread of the inferno, such as in Chicago and Boston for example.

It is stated in many historical accounts that two-thirds of Chicago consisted of wooden structures, yet browsing through pictures of Chicago from 1870, the year prior to the great fire, we see endless city streets lined with large and beautifully constructed brick buildings.

Photographs of Boston before the great fire also portray a cityscape of impressive brick buildings.

Historical records of the Boston inferno however, recounts the use of explosives to blow up buildings in the path of the fire in an attempt to create a firewall to prevent further spreading. The careless use of explosives apparently injured civilians, and the flaming debris only helped to propagate the fire.

It is also stated that the gas lines used to supply fuel to street lamps were not shut off, and the fuel still running through the lines were ignited by the flames and not only helped fuel the fire, but also caused explosions throughout parts of the city.

Considering the inconsistencies in our historical records, and the odd similarities between cities that have been leveled by explosives and others that have been destroyed by fires, we could also postulate that these cities were purposefully destroyed by explosives, and such as in the case of the Boston fire, the exploding gas lines and the explosives used to build the firewall may simply have been used as a scapegoat to cover its deliberate destruction.

Pictures may be our windows to the past, but they often tell tales which do not correlate with written accounts.

It is very odd to examine certain photographs taken of cities around the world in the 19th century where the streets are virtually devoid of any human presence. There are no horses, carts or any sign of activity anywhere in the streets. Yet photographs taken of these same areas just a few years later are teeming with life and activity.

In order to appreciate the scope of this subject, I suggest the reader visit Jon Levi's YouTube channel and watch some of his many videos. – https://www.youtube.com/@jonlevichannel/videos

There seems to be no rational explanations to justify this phenomenon, other than considering that these cities were already built and subsequently re-populated.

It would be reasonable to assume that our photographic records are accurate, as we would also assume that photo manipulation techniques had not yet been developed during this technology's infancy. These presuppositions however, would be inaccurate, and the discrepancies lie in the way photographs were taken and processed during that era.

"When a picture is taken with a camera it is made upon a glass plate, which, after development, shows the object in shades of black and white inversely. This plate is called the negative, in which all little imperfections of the skin, together with the shadows, wrinkles and facial blemishes, are necessarily exaggerated, and must be overcome by hand work in order to produce a correct and pleasing picture. It is to improve the picture by removing and softening these blemishes that the plate is sent to the   "re-toucher," who works upon the negative itself with fine implements."[58] (p. 6)

In other words, all photos of the era were touched-up and manipulated as a necessary component to a finished product.

Therefore, many tricks were used to manipulate the photos, of which some were meant to compensate for inherent camera limitations, and others used to blatantly fabricate entire scenes.

When taking a photograph of a cityscape for example, setting the aperture on the camera to be able to let in enough light to capture the buildings in the foreground, would cause the bright sky background to become overexposed, creating the vanilla sky effect. Photographers were able to compensate for this effect, by taking two separate photographs… one, focused on the cityscape, and one with a lowered aperture setting to capture the bright sky in the background. The two glass negatives were then layered together to form one single image, with the cityscape and sky both clearly visible.

This technique was commonly used at the time.

An avid postcard collector from British Columbia named James Brouwer, noticed a peculiar phenomenon as he was browsing through his collection of over 11,000 postcards, and discovered what has been dubbed "the mystery of the same sky postcards". Many of the photographs printed on the postcards had the exact same sky in the background.

Dexter Press Inc., one of the world's largest manufacturers of picture postcards, were in fact re-using the same background repeatedly throughout their processing.

Photo montages however, were not limited to just two photographs. Several glass negatives could be utilized to create elaborate forgeries.

"The two Ways of Life" was a famous Victorian photo montage produced by Oscar Rejlander in 1857, which combined over thirty negatives to produce the image.

In the 1860's, a phenomenon known as spirit photography was made famous by a photographer named William Mumler. He developed a double exposure processing technique that could introduce ghostly figures alongside living subjects, which he would then claim to be the spirits of dead loved ones trying to communicate with the people featured in the photographs. He was later exposed as a fraud.

Developers also used many other methods of photo manipulation such as etching, retouching, penciling and painting, which enabled them to alter photos to any envisioned outcome. They could remove people from photographs, add clothing, perform alterations to faces and bodies, remove furniture, alter landscapes, remove heads and bodies and replace them with the heads or bodies from other people, and virtually fabricate almost any optical representation imaginable.

There are countless examples of famous pictures being sold to the public as proof of historical accounts, when in fact, are complete forgeries. To gain insight on this subject, you may review a video titled "Old World Photoshop: Vanilla Skies, Early Photo Manipulation and Compositing Unveiled" by Shane St Pierre, or visit Stuffed Beagle's YouTube channel. Links below.

https://www.bitchute.com/video/G7wrLyooCbRy/

https://m.youtube.com/@stuffedbeagle/videos

Photographic manipulation also played a key role in helping to perpetuate the myth that our present technological advancements stem from innovations developed during the industrial revolutions.

This fabricated historical narrative, and the new paradigm for the future was then introduced to the world through our educational foundations and the control of information at all levels, as well as our scientific institutions displaying their latest innovations for the new world at the many world exhibitions held in various countries, notably from the mid-19th century to the early 20th century.

It is astounding to look at the technology being displayed at these World's Fairs. Large scale electrical lighting, moving sidewalks, the electrical speech machine (telephone), the Ferris wheel, the dishwasher, x-rays, ice cream cones, Cracker Jack popcorn, Aunt Jemima pancake mix, Wrigley's chewing gum, the hamburger, diet carbonated drinks, Shredded Wheat cereal, Nikola Tesla's alternating current technology, fluorescent light bulbs, spray painting, the fax machine, zippers, the television, live broadcasting, and a host of other technologies that were to be the cultural foundation of today's society.

The exhibitions were composed of colossal buildings, statues, monuments, exhibition halls, green houses, displays, fountains, amusement parks, restaurants, gift shops and court yards… built in an impossible timeframe… with a large portion of the structures either torn down, destroyed by fire, or tragically demolished after just a few months of operation, leaving but a few buildings, of which some are still standing today.

The awe-inspiring majesty of some of the structures used for the exhibitions cannot be expressed by mere words, and I therefore strongly suggest that the reader gaze upon their magnificence through the many photographs available on the internet. A few select pictures from the World's Columbian Exposition is also available in the "Old World" section of my website – pendulumsofpower.com.

Below is a short list of some of the more notable exhibitions featuring remarkable structures.

1851 – The Great Exhibition of the Works of Industry of All Nations – Hyde Park, London, United Kingdom, featuring the 990,000 square foot Crystal Palace – known as the first World's Fair – 6 million visitors

1853 – Exhibition of the Industry of All Nations – New York City, featuring the New York Crystal Palace – 1.1 million visitors

1860 – Montreal Industrial Exhibition – Montreal, Quebec – also featuring an enormous Crystal Palace

1876 – Centennial International Exhibition – Philadelphia, Pennsylvania – first official World's Fair held in the United States – 10 million visitors

1889 – Exposition Universelle – Paris, France – the Eiffel Tower was the main attraction – 32 million visitors

1894 – California Midwinter International Exposition – San Francisco's Golden Gate Park – 2.5 million visitors

1901 – Pan-American Exposition – Buffalo, New York – 8 million visitors

1904 – Louisiana Purchase Exposition – St. Louis, Missouri – nearly 20 million visitors.

The World's Columbian Exposition of 1893 was one of history's largest World's Fair, in terms of grandeur. The fair-grounds were spread across 1,037 acres of land with the addition of Washington Park, and was comprised of 65,000 exhibits, 200 buildings, numerous walkways, including a moving sidewalk, the Columbian Intramural Railway (an electrically powered 6-mile-long elevated railway), canals and lagoons, a huge basin complemented by incredible fountains such as the Columbia fountain that shot streams of water 150 feet high, and statues adorning breathtaking landscape architecture. Eighty acres were dedicated for the midway Plaisance, distinguished by a giant 264-foot-high Ferris wheel towering over countless concession stands, gift shops and restaurants with a combined seating capacity of 7,000, and the fair-grounds had a combined ability to feed 60,000 people an hour. There were gondolas traveling the canals, and life size replicas of Christopher Columbus' three ships – the Santa Clara, the Pinta and the Santa Maria.

The popular midway Plaisance was a huge amusement park with a zoo, balloon rides, a natatorium, large models of the Eiffel Tower, Blarney Castle, and St. Peter's Basilica, as well as a street in Cairo, a house of mirrors, a wax museum, endless souvenir stands, and much more. The highlight however, was the giant Ferris Wheel.[60] (p. 18)

The fourteen main "Great buildings" surrounded a giant reflective pool called the Grand Basin, and were built on an enormous scale.

With a volume of over 300 billion cubic feet, the Manufacturers and Liberal Arts Building was the largest building in the world at the time, and would be ranked second in volume on the list of the largest buildings in the world, were it still standing today. It measured 1,687' x 787', and had an astounding 44 acres of space for exhibits. The central hall had a roof span of 354' without supporting pillars, was 212' in height, and could seat a staggering 300,000 people.

Attracting over 27 million visitors, the fair became the location for the first large scale display of AC power that was going to shape the future of mankind. Backed by George Westinghouse, Nikola Tesla's new technology stole the show, as the fair's visitors were astounded by the nightly display of approximately one hundred and thirty thousand incandescent light bulbs that adorned the buildings surrounding the fair-grounds.

The Power House for the fair was located in Machinery Hall, which housed the largest boiler room in the world, containing

60 coal powered steam engines which operated 127 dynamos to produce a total of approximately 20,000 horse-power.

Additional power was produced by the 2000 horse-power Reynolds quadruple compound expansion engine, the Corliss engine producing 1400 horse-power, several engines similar to the Centennial Corliss, and numerous 1,000 horse-power engines.[59]

[59] *is a reference with a link to the Official Guide to the World's Columbian Exposition, and is itself 206 pages.*

Power requirements to operate lights, motors, pumps, elevators, the elevated railway, electric fountains, search lights, and a plethora of other electrical needs for the fair, was partially distributed through an elaborate underground Electrical Subway.

The tunnels were outfitted with 6000 crossarms, 30,000 pins, 4,000 special 2-wire insulators and 20,000 regular glass insulators. It held and distributed 25 miles of power lines, 28 miles of lines for incandescent lighting, and 51 miles of arc wires.

Above the total of 104 miles of power lines, there were also telephone and telegraph cables, fire alarm wiring, and police signal wires.

We might expect that such an undertaking in the late 19th century would have spanned at least two decades. The planning and organization alone would have taken at least a couple of years. Yet once again, we are astounded by the magical construction abilities of the people of this era.

Chicago was selected to be the host city on February 25, 1890, yet was required to raise an extra five million dollars. According to Julie K. Rose, the fundraising restrictions were lifted on December 24, 1890, and only afterwards did the work begin to plan the exposition and select a location.[60] (p. 6-7)

The chosen site was the Jackson Park lagoon on the south side of Chicago, which made the construction process that much more difficult as the foundations for many of the structures… including some of the largest buildings ever built… had to be laid upon unstable, freshly excavated land in a swamp.

The initial dredging and filling work began in January or February of 1881, and over 460 acres of land in Jackson Park had to be raised by over six and a half feet, and interlaced with ponds and waterways.[61]

Once this operation was completed, then began the task of building the 200 structures needed for the fair, as well as the walkways, bridges, fountains, statues, the elevated railway, the moving sidewalk etc.

The construction process is somewhat vague, as photographic representation of the fair was regulated, and therefore limited to the designated photographer, Charles Dudley Arnold. His pictures are published in a book called "Constructing the Fair", authored by himself and Peter Bacon Hales.

We are therefore limited to drawings and paintings, which are inadmissible as evidence, and the photographs produced by Charles Arnold, which raise more questions than they answer.

As it is common in construction photos of the era, we are often shown pictures of mostly finished buildings with scaffolding built around the structure, which could be indicative of a face-lift in progress, rather than a construction process.

Considering the number of workers which were employed to build the site… 12,000 to 40,000 depending on the source… other than staged photographs, there are rarely more than a few people randomly standing around in the picture, certainly not indicative of an immense crew frantically trying to finish the construction of so many structures in an impossible time frame.

As the entire fair was torn down or destroyed afterwards, it is also plausible that photographs were taken of structures which were being dismantled, and falsified as construction photos.

Combined with photo-manipulation techniques, as we know were available at the time, it was not beyond feasibility to fabricate the entire construction process of the fair.

What is even more vague regarding the construction, is the complexities surrounding the foundational work of the structures, however, we may get an idea of the challenges they would have faced, by examining the construction of the Ferris wheel.

The foundation consisted of eight concrete piers, 20' x 20' x 35', rested upon steel beams which were laid atop piles which were driven 32' deep, through water saturated sand. As this work had to be accomplished during one of the worst winters in Chicago history, steam had to be pumped in twenty-four hours a day to prevent frost build-up and allow the concrete to settle and dry. The piers then had to support the large towers that held up the 45' long, 71-ton axle, the 250' wheels, and the thirty-six, 27' x 13' x 9' passenger cars. Further questions arise when considering the immense size and weight of such materials needed for not only the Ferris wheel, but for the massive structures being built throughout the fairgrounds, and especially those being built around the Grand Basin. Massive steel beams and other construction materials had to be brought in and installed on a foundation of sand that when disturbed, would often become as soft as quicksand.[62, 63]

In a report regarding the landscape architecture of Jackson Park, consulting architect Frederick Law Olmsted outlines the challenges of transforming this sand filled marsh into a beautifully landscaped park, remarking that weather conditions such as rain and floods, as well as the movements of the sandy bottom due to underground springs, and the two feet thick sheet of ice that would be present until late spring, had sometimes caused the newly formed banks to slip off into the water, stating that he had lost thousands of aquatic plants due to this problem.[64 (p. 153)]

Faced with daunting time restraints, Olmsted submitted a pencil drawn sketch of the proposed plot on brown paper, which was adopted by the board on December 1st, 1890. The massive task began with the collection of tens of thousands of aquatic plants, hand-picked from the wild, and the planting of hundreds of thousands of herbaceous plants, willows, ferns, irises, and various types of perennials, which by the end, added to a total of over a million plants transplanted to the site.[64 (p. 152-153)]

This massive endeavor would have been undertaken during the summer of 1891 and 1892, as the fair opened in May of 1893, and the landscaping plan was adopted in December of 1890.

However, we can see that this "plan of the Exposition" was adopted before the site had even been chosen. The Presidential Proclamation officially recognizing Chicago as the host of the fair was not issued until December 24, 1890. The construction of the buildings and the choice of a site had yet to be determined, according to Julie K. Rose.

This pencil-drawn, brown-paper plot was not the only "sketchy" anomaly in the timeline. We must consider that not only did the landscaping and construction had to be accomplished before the opening of the fair in May of '93, but the construction process would have required completion, allowing enough time to set up the 65,000 exhibits, the 60 steam engines and 127 dynamos, the 4000 water closets, the concession stands and restaurants, the wiring and installation of over 120,000 light bulbs, the building of bridges, walkways, moving sidewalks, 6 miles of elevated rail lines etc., and we could continue indefinitely, listing the myriad of supplies and materials necessary for hosting such an event.

To suggest that this massive undertaking was accomplished in the span of 2 short years is preposterous. It would have taken at least that long to simply plan the event.

In more realistic terms, let us then suggest that the White City was already built. It would be much more plausible to believe that it took two years to set up the exhibits and organize the fair to accommodate the millions of visitors which were to attend in the coming months after its opening.

With the infrastructure already in place, the tasks would have consisted of getting the fair-grounds stocked with the needed supplies, setting up the exhibits and gift shops, making sure the generators, rail cars, midways and electrical systems were functioning, repairing any damaged infrastructure, organizing the exhibition and cleaning up the site… which in itself would have already been a monumental task.

Such a speculation therefore suggests that the entire fair-grounds, including all the infrastructure and technology being displayed, was merely a re-branding of the already existing framework of the old world.

Curiously, there were some World's Fairs which hosted exhibits which were, by today's standards, questionable to say the least.

Strangely enough, an American Obstetrician named Martin Couney developed incubators for pre-mature babies, and for a small fee you could get a glance at these incubator babies, on display at several fairs in what were called "Infantoriums". He began exhibiting his incubator babies in 1896, and continued his sideshow attraction up until the mid-1940's in the United States.

We might conceptualize this endeavor in the context of a new world being created, using massive amounts of children, shipped and distributed throughout the entire continent.

You may or may not have heard of the orphan trains?

Records indicate that around this era, hundreds of thousands of children were being sent to cities worldwide, and adopted by families in an effort to populate our countries with a fresh set of working hands.

Children were taken from unwed mothers and families who apparently could not afford to raise their own. Large insane asylums were built to house distressed parents who did not agree with the new system being introduced. It would also explain the curious necessity for the numerous orphanages operating at the time.

You can see the picture unfolding in a new light when viewed through the narrative of a new world vision. An era where the old technology was to be replaced with a rebranded, patented technology, stamped with a price tag. A mechanism of control for the new world order.

It is said that an entire history can be re-written within three generations, but a society with a significant population of orphaned children could be re-educated within one generation.

The world we see today is a product of this re-written history, and the borrowed technologies are but the tools used to implement this new fascist world regime.

Since the advent of the printing press and the first television newscasts, the media has always been a tool of the ruling oligarchy to shape and mold public opinion… and a true "free press" has never truly existed.

Although we could argue that the internet became a tool where one could share their thoughts unhindered by censorship, can we truly state that this platform offers such a benefit, when we consider that its structure was designed, built, and distributed by the very people who have taken control of all informational platforms, and are responsible for the eradication of civil liberties worldwide?

As we already know, there is a certain percentage of the population that cannot be fooled by their deceptions, and we can use Nikola Tesla as an example of the methods used to lead these inquisitive minds astray, and how the internet was developed in part as a tool to mis-direct truth-seekers away from the truth.

As Tesla's contributions were never made part of our school curriculum, he was virtually unknown to most until the internet made it possible for the world to learn of his astounding achievements. Yet most people today are more likely to ascribe the name Tesla to solar panels and electric cars.

Although seemingly branded as new technology, the first electric cars actually made their appearance in 1828, and the first practical EV's, invented by William Morrison, made their debut in the late 1880's. According to Arthur H. Matthews, (Nikola Tesla's last known assistant), Tesla had invented an electric car in 1897, and Matthews stated in an interview that it was powered by a primary battery that could run the car for five hundred miles before being attended to. He goes on to say that "some time in the future somebody will no doubt build this Tesla electric car." – Arthur H. Matthews – Nikola Tesla's Assistant – https://www.patreon.com/posts/arthur-h-nikola-40893482?l=de

FLASHBACK…

I was working as an EFP audio tech on a series profiling interesting people and places across central and western Canada, and the featured guest in one particular episode, brought us to the homestead of a man who owned land that was rich in oil deposits, and to his good fortune, also held the mineral rights to his property.

Suffice it to say that his wealth allowed him to live the life of his choosing, and being fascinated with antiquities, he spent a great deal of his time collecting vast amounts of historical artifacts. His collection included an impressive inventory of vintage cars, trucks and farm machinery… most of which were kept in a large heated shop.

One item in particular… a two-seater from the twenties… caught my attention, as it did not seem to have an engine bay. To my astonishment, the man pointed out that it was an electric car. I had no idea that electric vehicles were even conceived of in that era.

I was perplexed as to how this technology had not been improved upon in over seventy years. The modern electric vehicles that I was aware of at the time (the nineties), were still in their infancy, and I dare say the science had regressed. This newly-found discovery was a clear indication to me that this technology was being purposely suppressed.

(End of Flashback)

If indeed, there exists a conspiracy to hide the old world and its technology, the narrative would have required a method to justify the newly fabricated history, chronicling a period of new innovations which were to shape the future.

The pre-existing technology which was to be re-introduced to the public, had to be attributed to such individuals which would become the figure-heads… the "inventors" of these "new" innovations. Some however, might have been recruited for their adept scientific propensities, as they were able to decipher the technology and reverse engineer its designs so as to be able to re-draft, re-patent, and re-build these engineering marvels for future use.

Tesla, having been granted approximately 300 patents, branded as the father of modern technology, was later discredited as a mad scientist when trying to display some of his more revolutionary innovations, as they were not befitting this new world paradigm… such as wireless transmission of electricity which exposed the true electro-magnetic construct of this realm.

We could now put a face to the incredible technology that was to shape our world. A genius of such proportion was not only a plausible candidate to accredit with such marvels, but was also perfectly suited to be branded as the mad scientist type, producing technology such as wireless electrical distribution, mind control scalar wave weapons and "death rays", which could then be purposefully denigrated as pseudo-science and withdrawn from society.

We must also consider that this powerful technology could have also been used to cause the worldwide "mud flood". Tesla did mention that some of his innovations would be able to resonate the earth and cause natural disasters such as earthquakes.

Truth-seekers were now provided with a conspiracy to hide free energy, and a logical explanation to substantiate the inventor's untimely fate, concluding that he was de-funded, cast away and written out of the history books as a way to suppress his works from the public, as the ruling class did not want to promote a system that would provide energy to the world which could not be monetized.

The internet therefore, could be venerated as the wonderful tool that helped to expose the conspiracy, when in fact it was merely being used to misdirect the public in order to hide the true conspiracy, which was the concealment of the old world and its technology, and the calamity which precipitated its annihilation.

Tesla's legacy has been forever memorialized through countless articles written in various newspapers and magazines, transcripts of his many lectures, hundreds of books… 28 of which were written by Tesla himself…, websites dedicated to his life and achievements, as well as the numerous patents that he had filed in 26 countries around the world.

Considering this man's vast influence on our present technology, it is curious that not a single one of his lectures or interviews have ever been made available on film or video, and not a single moving picture exists of him working in his laboratory or experimenting with his inventions. Of the few photographs taken of him throughout his lifetime, there is not a single photograph of him actually holding a tool in his hand, or in the process of building any apparatus pertaining to any of his inventions.

Everything we know of this man's accomplishments can only be corroborated through written texts and eye witness accounts.

Although I believe it would be imprudent to say that the transcripts of interviews and lectures were not the true accounts of Tesla himself, we may consider that the numerous inventions and patents which he filed may have been; a) Written by someone other than Tesla… b) Written by Tesla, who reverse engineered the existing technology, or… c) A re-written transcript of the existing blueprints and design schematics which may have been made available to him and subsequently destroyed or concealed from the public.

If Tesla was indeed, not the man responsible for the conceptualization and construct of all the inventions attributed to his name, how was he able to convincingly represent himself to the public and the scientific community as a knowledgeable and competent scientist capable of such innovative ingenuity? Here is where may lie Tesla's true genius.

Being gifted with a photographic memory, Tesla had the ability to commit entire books to memory. He lived a more reclusive life, which allowed him to devote much of his time to the accumulation of knowledge, and combined with the fact that he was also a fascinating story teller, it was well within his abilities to be able to embody the role of a genius, mad scientist.

This title would come to be a useful tool in this deception, as unconventional viewpoints or misunderstood scientific interpretations could be attributed to his eccentric perspectives.

"Before I put a sketch on paper, the whole idea is worked out mentally. In my mind, I change the construction, make improvements, and even operate the device. Without ever having drawn a sketch, I can give the measurements of all parts to workmen, and when completed these parts will fit, just as certainly as though I had made accurate drawings. It is immaterial to me whether I run my machine in my mind or test it in my shop."[65] (p. 18)

Therefore, such an ability would have provided him with a perfect alibi to account for the lack of hand written notes and diagrams that would have presumably been drawn from his countless inventions.

However, several files regarding Tesla were released by the FBI between 2016 and 2018, which allude to Tesla having a multitude of written records of his inventions.

"In past conversations TESLA has told FITZGERALD that he has some 80 trunks in different places containing manuscripts and plans having to do with experiments conducted by him."[66] (p. 2-3)

These documents however were quickly taken away shortly after his death.

"On January 7, 1943, SAVA KOSANOVICH, GEORGE CLARK, who is in charge of the Museum and Laboratory for RCA, and KENNETH SWEZEY… went to TESLA's rooms in the New Yorker and with the assistance of a lock smith broke into a safe which TESLA had in his rooms and in which he kept some of his valuable papers, including important electrical formulae, designs, etc. These papers were taken from the safe."[66] (p. 3)

The final resting place for most of his possessions became the basement of the Nikola Tesla Museum in Belgrade, Serbia, where they have apparently stored more than 160,000 original documents, 2000 books and journals, over 1,200 exhibits, 1,500 photographs and original photo plates, and over 1,000 plans and drawings made by Tesla. Surprisingly, very little is actually on display.

If there are indeed over 1,500 photographs of Tesla, why are so few available to the public?

What kind of books and journals did Tesla possess?

What constituted such an impressive number of "original documents"? Tesla could not possibly have produced so many documents. To put this in perspective… assuming each "document" consisted of only one page… if he consistently wrote 10 pages every single day, it would take approximately 44 years to complete 160,000 pages.

When could he possibly have found the time to attend to his studies, read his books, work on his inventions, write hundreds of patents, complete his 1,000 plans and designs, write and perform lectures etc.?

Perhaps we may consider that these were simply the documents. plans, designs and blueprints written by the true creators of this technology, which were made available to him to perpetuate his role as the genius inventor, and were simply reclaimed and safely stored away after his death.

It would also explain the hasty retreat of his belongings at the first sign of his passing, to ensure that none of his records would end up in the "wrong hands" and risk exposing the deception.

It is a common belief that Tesla spent his final years in seclusion, in a cheap apartment in New York City, previously having been evicted from several other hotels in the city.

There are also allegations that he had to resort to selling his "death ray" in order to pay debts, and apparently had to sell the Wardenclyffe Tower in order to settle a $20,000 bill accrued at the Waldorf-Astoria in 1915.

To put things in perspective, $20,000 in 1915 is the equivalent of approximately $500,000 today. I think it would be fair to presume that there isn't a single hotel in existence today that would allow anyone to rack up a half-million-dollar bill before evicting them out of their establishment. Yet Tesla was able to get away with amassing large amounts of debt in one hotel after another, in the same city, for forty consecutive years?

In actual fact, during the last forty-three years of his life, Tesla made his residence in many of New York's finest hotels.

The Pennsylvania Hotel – When built in 1919, it was the largest hotel in the world, and accommodated such guests as Fidel Castro and Harry Houdini. Biological warfare scientist, Frank Olson, suspiciously plunged to his death from a window at the hotel after being secretly dosed with LSD, as part of the CIA's MK Ultra mind control project.

The Governor Clinton Hotel – A luxurious hotel with an underground passage that led to the Pennsylvania Railroad Terminal.

The Waldorf-Astoria Hotel – A lavish hotel, known as the first of New York's "Palace Hotels". Accommodated such high-profile guests as Queen Elizbeth II, Ava Gartner, John Wayne, Marilyn Munroe, Tony Bennett, Judy Garland and Frank Sinatra. Beneath the building was a secret railway known as Track 61.

The St. Regis Hotel – Was described by the press as being the most richly furnished and opulent hotel in the world.

The Marguery Hotel – A six-building luxury complex.

The New Yorker – Once the tallest building in New York, it was a stunningly beautiful hotel, forty-three stories high, and had its own power generator, a hospital with an operating room, an indoor ice rink, a secretary on every floor, an internal radio system connected to every room, and a subterranean tunnel that led to the Pennsylvania Station.[67]

"Throughout the 1940's and 1950's, the hotel was among New York's most fashionable. In the building's heyday, it hosted many popular Big Bands, such as Benny Goodman and Tommy Dorsey, while notable figures such as Spencer Tracy, Joan Crawford, and Fidel Castro stayed there. Inventor Nikola Tesla spent the last ten years of his life in near-seclusion in Suite 3327, where he died…"[68]

Hardly a picture of man left destitute and penniless. Let us instead, paint Tesla's portrait onto the canvas of this new world deception.

A genius in his own right, an avid reader with a photographic memory, a polyglot who could speak eight languages, a businessman, a poet, a writer, a philosopher, a mystic, a great orator and storyteller, elegant and stylish, Tesla was the perfect candidate to recruit as the figurehead of a brilliant intellectual scientist in this new historical narrative.

He was provided with access to already existing electrical machinery, laboratories, power-plants and various technological wonders… supplied with all the necessary designs and blueprints to examine, learn, and memorize as the script to his part in this theatrical piece, subsequently becoming a magnate in the scientific community and in the general public through substantial media support, his scientific lectures, and demonstrations of these incredible electrical devices in such places as the World's Columbian Exhibition, astonishing millions with his captivating stories.

He was well paid, and lived a lavish life, receiving multiple awards and medals for his "achievements"… some of which were presented to him by royalty… was well known through his appearances in countless news articles and magazines, and contrary to the common story depicted of him in the latter part of his life as a destitute man, alone and forgotten, he lived in many of the finest hotels in New York, was visited frequently by renowned personalities and dignitaries of all walks of life, including his friend Mark Twain and King Peter of Yugoslavia, he threw yearly birthday parties in the grand ballrooms of the New Yorker, had yearly press conferences and lived up to his contractual obligations up until his death in 1943.

We must be cognizant of the fact that re-writing history required the collaboration of key people in various fields. Since the technology already existed, scientists, engineers and inventors such as Tesla, Edison, and Marconi were instrumental in helping to perpetuate the hoax. Since the cities were already built, financiers such as Westinghouse, Rockefeller and Morgan were a necessary component. Collaborators were also needed in the media and entertainment industries, politics, manufacturing and many other fields. Therefore, a "clique" is formed of people who are paid figureheads, actors, writers, architects, businessmen, and politicians who are all "in" on the game, and understand each other's role in the re-writing of our history. If remained unverified, such as in Tesla's case, these misrepresentations can be forever perpetuated and sold as the truth.

Considering the grandeur of the establishments in which Tesla made his residence, the proprietors would have consequently been part of the same clique of fraudsters, and have known of Tesla's involvement. Their role was to accommodate this brother-in-arms and make sure he was well taken care of until his passing. His debts were inconsequential, and his "unfortunate tale" was simply maintained as a cover.

In this theatrical performance, no actor will dare expose another as they would only be revealing their own treachery, and be faced with the harsh consequences. The entire apparatus is so all-encompassing that the majority of the audience will simply acquiesce in ignorant conformity and participate without question, as the entire game is too large to comprehend and too well funded and organized to criticize. The few that are courageous enough to challenge the system are either discredited by the establishment, or strategically eliminated if they become too large of a threat.

A new world is then created, built upon a contrived history, and the old-world metamorphoses into myths and legends.

It does become obvious at some point that certain truths are being withheld from the public through various means, such as the manipulation of search engine algorithms.

If for example, you type in "covid does not exist" on a common search engine site, your suggestions will be limited to websites, articles, blogs and videos that oppose this idea and/or belittle and condemn any who entertain such "unscientific" and "dangerous" conspiracy theories, therefore quickly dissuading any new truth seeker.

I was myself subject to such fascist censorship of information when I received an email from YouTube Community Guidelines informing me that they had removed one of my videos, as it violated their "medical misinformation policy". The following is a quote from the email.

"YouTube doesn't allow content that disputes local health authority or World Health Organization (WHO) information by explicitly denying the existence of COVID -19 or its severity."

In other words, we are not allowed to express any facts or opinions that contradict government or corporate edicts and positions regarding this subject. If free speech is limited to pre-approved governmental scrutinization of allowable content, then it is obviously censorship, and fascist in nature.

This fact alone speaks volumes as there is no other point to such tactics, other than trying to hide something truthful, that could expose a lie.

However, we may consider that there is a point where the information is inconsequential, as the larger picture is the complete integration of our lives into the medium in which the information is being exchanged.

Our means of communication, banking, socializing, entertainment and work, have been digitized into this grid, where we are tracked and monitored twenty-four seven.

No one escapes the constant and total manipulation and use of personal information and data.

The dystopian future outlined in the United Nations Agenda 21, can no longer be ignored as outlandish theories, as this new world of mass censorship and loss of liberties has now been brought to light thanks to this recent pandemic of lies, instilling fear into the hearts of the common folk.

The World Economic Forum openly details its vision of smart cities populated by a new and improved kind of genetically modified human being labeled "human 2.0", a patented product owned by these controllers, to be used and abused at their discretion.

A.I. technology, being sold to the populace as a great tool for the advancement of our society, has its roots buried deep in this diabolical agenda. An agenda that strips every human of all autonomy, freedom, ownership and choice, where your own thoughts and actions can be manipulated and controlled, and your memories erased and replaced. Total and complete hegemonic dominance over the minds of all human 2.0's.

The manipulation and deletion of history is not as difficult as one might think.

I was having a conversation regarding environmental disasters with an intelligent nineteen-year-old high school graduate, and I mentioned the Gulf War. To my surprise, he was completely unaware that this war had even taken place.

Granted, he wasn't born when the incident happened, but he was certainly aware of both world wars and the Vietnam conflict… which lends me to wonder… why was he not aware of the war that was responsible for creating the largest man-made environmental disaster in world history?

This incident was swept clean out of the school curriculum and out of the history books of high school academia, eradicating its existence from the minds of our youth, in the span of just one generation.

A large percentage of our true history is completely omitted from our academia, and the rest constitutes misrepresentations and fabrications. It is more likely that what we have been taught as myths and lore, is a closer representation of our real history.

The Greeks, Hebrews, Sumerians, Aztecs, Mesopotamians, Egyptians, Indians, Israelites, Chinese, Japanese, and virtually every culture in ancient history, have all recorded very similar ideologies regarding the creation and history of the earth, along with models depicting the environment in which we live.

Common, are seen the terms "gods", "giants" and "titans".

Common, are seen megalithic structures, having been built around their cultures.

Common, are seen organized and structured societies.

Common, are seen advanced scientific and engineering marvels.

It was no small feat of engineering and construction mastery to design and build the monolithic structures and statues that are found around the world today. Modern engineers are incapable of building such structures with the technology available today, and dumbfounded as to its method of construction.

Using the great pyramids as an example, accepted science offers this as a theory: The blocks used to build the pyramids of Giza were cut out of solid stone, using copper chisels and rocks, dragged across the desert using logs and hemp ropes, positioned into place using poles and ramps, (which would have been more of an accomplishment than building the pyramids themselves), using the labor of thousands of slaves.

Or, we could entertain the hypothesis proposed by Joseph Davidovits, a Chemical Engineer from France.

Davidovits suggests that instead of cutting blocks out of solid stone and hauling them at great distances, to then be stacked upon each other to form a pyramid, they were formed using a type of ancient concrete he calls geopolymer, and poured into wooden molds directly onto the pyramid.

This geopolymer concrete can be made using the natural limestone abundantly available on the Giza plateau, and mixing it with clay, water and lime… an alkaline activator that causes the mixture to solidify into solid stone.

This wet mixture could be easily manufactured and hauled to the pyramid using sacks carried on the backs of workers, and its construction would have required a fraction of the workforce estimated to have built the pyramids and other structures.

Once cured, the wooden molds were removed and rebuilt in position to make the next blocks, which could be poured to very accurate dimensions, and as the geopolymer would solidify against the adjacent blocks, joints would be perfectly butted together.

This theory however, does not tailor to the currently accepted model of human history and therefore, will not be acknowledged as a credible hypothesis.

This academia, self-proclaimed as the most technologically advanced, civilized, and "evolved" to have ever walked the earth, is incapable of understanding the technological accomplishments of ancient civilizations, and unwilling to entertain any alternative explanation which contradict their evolutionary model, but are willing to accept and fiercely defend the most outrageous and improbable of theories, simply because it suits their model.

The statistical probability of our ancient cultures, separated by un-crossable oceans and hundreds of years in time, developing the same megalithic construction methods and similar historical accounts without outside influence, is undoubtably very low… unless of course our ancestors did have the capability to communicate or cross the oceans.

We are therefore left to entertain three possibilities that may explain these historical anomalies; gods/giants, aliens from outer space, or that our ancestors were more intelligent and sophisticated than our history books will admit.

Approximately half of all the human beings in the world today now believe in the existence of extra-terrestrial life. Does this mean that they do indeed exist, because of "proof by popular belief"?

The fact remains, that there isn't one single piece of evidence to substantiate the space-aliens myth. There exists no proof that documented cases of abductions, sightings, cattle mutilations or crop circles, were actually carried out by aliens from another "planet".

The fact remains, that lifeforms of any kind have never been found to exist anywhere beyond the confines of this earth.

The fact remains, that extra-terrestrial beings are confined to Hollywood myths and NASA lore.

We do however, have thousands of years of literature handed down by our ancestors, depicting their versions of reality, which are also ironically labeled as myths and lore.

Are we then to believe that Cronos and Zeus actually existed, and are part of our true history?

Should we not consider that if we are impressionable enough to believe that aliens from outer space exist, it's no big leap of faith to believe that "gods" and giants could have existed. Our ancestors did religiously document their presence throughout thousands of years. They did not (*allowing room for interpretation*) document a history of creation and manipulation by aliens from outer space.

When examining magnificent ancient structures and temples such as the Temple of Bacchus at Baalbek in Lebanon, the temples at Karnak in Egypt, or the treasury at the ancient city of Petra in southern Jordan, we may be astonished at the immensity of its halls and doorways, yet could find context when considering that the immense size of these structures may have been designed to accommodate a race of giants/gods. Why would any human need to make doorways that exceed forty feet, or build such colossal structures all over the world?

The evidence of the presence of these giants not only lies in the megalithic structures they left behind, but can also be found in the enormous humanoid skeletal remains that have been discovered worldwide, and the numerous photographs taken of giants living in the late 19th and early 20th centuries.

Regardless of whom was responsible for building such structures, we must admit to a certain level of arrogance, when gazing in awe at the creations of our ancestors, as we mock their beliefs and dismiss them as myths and legends.

Would a human society, two thousand years into the future, mock our belief in space aliens? Would they mock our models and theories of creation? Would they assess our generation as being unevolved?

We can however, learn through these "myths" that the "gods" were the offspring of Titans.

The Titans were a gargantuan and powerful race of deities which ruled the earth during the Golden Age of creation.

They were also responsible for providing humanity with the knowledge to create fire, as well as instructing humanity on the fine arts of language, reading, writing, irrigation, philosophy, architecture, science, agriculture and war.

Wouldn't it be reasonable to consider that if Titans and "gods" did in fact walk among us in our distant past, they could have been the architects of the monolithic structures we still see standing today? Couldn't they have been the bridge that endowed the races of the world with similar knowledge and technology?

Is it possible that they still exist today? After all, they were considered immortal.

It's a matter of perspective…

An insect that has a lifespan of two days, will not perceive time in the same manner as a person with a lifespan of a hundred years. If it observes a person walk out the front door of their home, and come back the next day, from its perspective, that person will have been gone for half its life.

An immortal "god" that might have a lifespan of tens of thousands of years, could easily plot hundreds… even thousands of years in advance. They could master the art of deception and manipulate history to suit their needs.

Visions of the future, as were predicted by such prophets as Nostradamus and Edgar Cayce, could have instead just been the transcriptions of an already written future, had they been aware of the plot.

Do "gods" really exist?
Do "aliens" really exist?
Does "outer space" really exist?
Do "we" really exist?

It might sound silly, to contemplate our own existence. A more fitting question however should address the nature of the reality in which we "exist". If we define our "existence" according to the physical nature of our environment, we would have to define it in terms of our senses, which allow us to interact with our surroundings.

If you experiment by sitting down in a quiet environment, closing your eyes, and imagining yourself completely disconnected from all your senses, you enter into a world where your mind is your only companion.

If you cannot feel, taste, touch, see or hear the world around you, does the world around you exist?

Quantum physicists suggest that reality does not exist, until you give it your attention.[69]

If you were born without senses and kept alive in a hospital bed, what would you think about? Never, would you have been exposed to any kind of sensory stimulus. You would know nothing of birds and trees. You would know nothing of hot and cold, or up and down. You would not know the smell of fresh baked bread or the taste of chocolate. You would have never seen your own body or that of any other person. You would have never heard a single sound. You would have never learned a language and therefore would be unable to even speak to yourself.

How then can the mind even formulate a thought, if it has never been exposed to anything?

We must then postulate that the mind is therefore inexorably linked to the physical world, and cannot possibly be the source of consciousness. As a result, we must look outside of the physical nature of our environment to define our existence.

Chapter 10

THE NEW AGE AND SPIRITUALITY

Humanity is clearly not deficient in philosophical and spiritual ideologies, nor is it lacking interpretations of common religious tenets.

We may look back at the roots of our spiritual traditions however, and identify a common origin.

This innate human desire to answer the fundamental questions of existence has cultivated a slew of metaphysical doctrines to help guide us on our journey.

Many religious organizations are well-established to help people cope with the uncertainties and fears engendered by the inevitable end of our existence in this material world, and bring a sense of comfort and closure to those dealing with the hardships associated with the trials of life and the loss of loved ones.

Although we cannot deny the beneficial impacts that many religious organizations have had on countless people who were struggling with life's hardships, these human vulnerabilities may also be exploited by the dark forces of this world who feed upon the innocent and ignorant with ill intent.

Endowed with esoteric truths, these dark forces can easily coerce humanity towards pursuing a misguided spiritual path that only serves to diminish their potentiality and keep them trapped in the illusory world of duality, where they may paradoxically fuel the opposite of their intended objectives.

However, when faced with subjective matters of faith, one cannot readily be convinced by hard evidence, and must rely on personal convictions accrued through confidence in one's own creed, or trust in the interpretations and dictates of one's chosen religious institution.

Today, as we approach a significant crossroad in human development in this great cycle of life, the access to information afforded to us by technology has catapulted an interest in pursuing esoteric knowledge, and many have chosen to seek alternative viewpoints regarding scientific and spiritual matters, with the aim of expanding their consciousness beyond conventional belief systems, as one no longer need seek mystic gurus on the peaks of Tibetan mountains to find enlightenment.

This phenomenon has led to the considerable growth of what is typically branded as the "new age movement".

Upon extensive investigation, one may discover that these "new age" philosophies, compared with familiar religious beliefs, have common roots dating back millennia, stem from ancient texts of esoteric knowledge and wisdom, where no disassociation is made between science and spirituality.

These timeless teachings of the science of creation are today being confirmed through discoveries in the field of quantum physics, which purports to have found a link between thought and physical manifestation, and lends credence to the principles of the law of attraction.

"What we think we become." – *Buddha*

The law of attraction suggests that our outer reality is a manifestation of our inner thoughts and emotional state. For example; if one believes their life to be a constant struggle, and is absorbed in feelings of financial lack, their outer reality will reflect these beliefs. Similarly, if one believes themselves to be weak and sick, their body will begin to deteriorate.

There are countless examples of people having recovered from life threatening illnesses without the use of any treatments. This mind over matter technique has also been proven successful with the "placebo effect", whereas patients were administered "treatments" which consisted of simple sugar pills, but were made to believe they were powerful drugs and miraculously recovered from their illness.

This curious phenomenon inevitably led to the contemplation of the mind's true potential, and a re-examination of our spiritual teachings, which has helped to fuel this new age culture.

This online community of self-help gurus has had a profound impact on the lives of millions of people, offering methods for overcoming fear, anxiety, addiction, stress etc., and empowering many into creating for themselves, a life of love, abundance, and connection to their divine nature.

We may however feel obliged to challenge the motives and authenticity of those who have made millions from their followers and live a life of abundance and luxury, while preaching the virtues of a faith that does not align with such egotistical pursuits.

In ancient Tibetan spiritual traditions, utilizing these spiritual powers to attract wealth or personal gain was considered black magic.

"Whenever any spiritual aspirant was found to be attempting to use spiritual or mental power to attract wealth, possessions, or material and personal fulfillment, he was expelled in disgrace from the temple, the monastery, the ashram, or the spiritual community. It has always been understood that true progress in the spiritual life and the path of inner development and unfoldment of the soul are dependent upon selflessness, altruism, humility, and living solely to be of benefit to mankind…"[70]

It is believed that desire is the root of all suffering, and the eradication of all desire is the only true spiritual path. However, we must consider that without the desire to eat, drink and survive, there can be no life. Furthermore, without the desire to follow the spiritual path, one cannot learn to overcome desire.

If one endeavors to be of service to humanity however, one must be in a position to be able to be of service. A person who is needy, greedy, angry, jealous and anxious is an energy vampire that only serves to strip others of their energy and can be of no real service. Therefore, using spiritual powers to gain strength, wisdom, wealth and self-mastery will, with noble intention, allow one to be overflowing with giving energy and have more time to devote to this cause.

But how does one come to understand spiritual "truths"? How can one trust knowledge that cannot be described by mere words? Where did this information originate? How did the sages of old come to the conclusion that the only true spiritual path is living solely for the benefit of others?

Hidden away in remote temples and ashrams, there are certain spiritual wisdoms that are kept secret from the public. How then can they describe themselves as being of service to humanity, when they keep themselves hidden away in remote areas of the world, while hoarding knowledge and meditating incessantly in isolation?

We could say that this practice is eerily reminiscent of the Jesuit's concealment of valuable records and texts, and akin to the ambiguous rituals performed in their secret temples.

Although a life of devotion to one's creed breeds its own challenges, this evasion of human interaction will keep one ignorant of the true struggles and tests that build inner strength, and can be interpreted as a form of selfishness to one's own self-fulfilling purpose.

It is not the sages themselves who have ventured out into the world to spread goodwill and sacred wisdom, it is the adventurers who have dared to seek out this wisdom and took measures to share it with the world. Although these truths might not have been discovered, were it not for the sages' dedication and devotion to this path.

Are we then to be advised in worldly affairs, by those who have chosen to retreat from the world?

Naturally, we cannot dismiss the possibility that the reasons behind the secrecy may have meaning beyond our comprehension, but we must also question the source of this knowledge.

According to Helena Blavatsky, founder of the Theosophical society, the Law of Theosophy was not only "wisdom of the gods", it was "wisdom possessed by the gods".

Who… or what… were these "gods"? We cannot forget that the gurus who have discovered these "truths" are but human beings with the same frailties and limitations imposed upon everyone else, and may be misled through inherent human ignorance.

How was this knowledge transmitted by these "gods" to humankind? Was it delivered in person at a time when it is said that these "gods" walked among us in this world? Was it transmitted telepathically through such practices as channeling, or mediumship? How were they to trust this wisdom when communicated in such a fashion, and who or what exactly was transferring this information? Why were they referred to as "gods"? As any other label, "gods" is just a word used to describe an indescribable phenomenon. Did these communicators label themselves as "gods"?

Theosophy suggests that channeled entities might be deceased individuals who are trapped in the astral plane, astral shells or Kama Rupas, Elemental beings, or "Evil human beings, in some cases belonging to what has been called the Dark Brotherhood or Black Lodge or 'Brothers of the Shadow,' whose intention is simply to destroy the usefulness and potential benefit that spiritual people can bring to the world and to deceive, to delude, and to divert people's attention away from solid spiritual truth and into the chaotic realms of sheer fantasy and fiction. Such beings as these will use anyone they can – and especially voluntary victims – to fulfil their aims and will have no qualms about passing themselves off as holy Masters, archangels, or as Buddha himself!"[71]

It was forewarned by Blavatsky and the Masters credited with the inspiration behind her writings, that there would be a time in the 20th century where many would be deceived by such entities, influencing humanity through the practice of channeling, or mediumship.

There are many authors in this new age culture which speak of being possessed by certain entities. These authors, claiming only to be a vessel for what they have respectively described as demons, gods, angels, aliens, Pleiadeans, spirits, Ascended Masters, Buddha, Krishna, Jesus, Saint Germain and many others.

The product of their messages has evolved into a vast network of well-intentioned "lightworkers" who believe that the world is presently surrounded by beings from other planets, and are part of the "Galactic Federation", or "Ashtar Command", here to help humanity transition to higher levels of spiritual existence.

An American woman named Doris Ekker, purporting to channel entities such as Gyeorgos Ceres Hatonn, Ishtar and Sananda, to name a few, transcribed their messages in over thirteen thousand pages, printed in roughly one-hundred and fifteen booklets called the Phoenix Journals, which helped to propagate what has been labeled the "I am" movement.

The term "I am", refers to a state of one's natural divine connection, or soul, which transcends the mind's perception of self, or ego, and is also widely used by self-help authors and speakers such as Esther Hicks, Eckart Tolle, Neville Goddard and Wayne Dyer, as a means to describe this divine nature which permeates our being, and also to create affirmations to guide our lives in accordance with our desires.

Esther Hicks, a channeler for what she describes as a group of non-physical entities she names "Abraham", has made millions with her teachings and courses, as well as multiple New York Times best-selling books, and appearances in the movie The Secret and on the Oprah Winfrey show.

Oprah has been promoting this new age concept since at least 1988, when she invited Penny Rubin on her show, a woman who claimed that she could channel at will, a spirit she named Mafu.

Another popular channeler named JZ Knight, claiming to be a channel for "Ramtha", an Ascended Master, has made millions through her teachings at Ramtha's School of Enlightenment, and has appeared on Larry King Live, the Merv Griffin Show, and the movie What the Bleep do we Know is largely based on her teachings.

Channeling however, is not limited to self-help gurus and Lightworkers. It is also common practice in our modern entertainment industry.

Why do most entertainers in the upper echelons of the entertainment industry affirm to letting themselves be possessed by entities from the unseen realms of existence? Could it be part of their contractual obligations? The term "we sold our soul for rock 'n' roll" may have more meaning than one might expect.

In a 2004 "60 Minutes" interview, Bob Dylan was asked why he is still out there entertaining at his age, and he responded by saying that he was holding up his end of a bargain that he had made with the "Chief Commander" of the earth and from a world we can't see.[72]

Why would he make such a statement? We must remember that this was not an extract of Bob joking around with his buddies back stage before a concert… this was an admission made on the most popular television news program in history.

The entertainment industry is controlled at the very top by the Jesuits, and if they are to fund and promote your career through their vast network of resources, you must sign a contract and abide by your contractual obligations.

Many artists will admit to having "sold their soul", through lucrative record contracts signed in their own blood, in return for fame and fortune.

As the Jesuits admit to worshipping "Lucifer" as their "god", perhaps it is nothing less than a Faustian bargain… aka a "deal with the Devil".

But who, or what, is "Lucifer"?

Like any other word, it has the meaning to which is impressed upon it in written or spoken language.

Is it a reference to a "fallen angel" described in religious texts? Translated from Latin, it means "light bringer", or "light bearer", and has also been associated with Venus, the "morning star", or "son of the dawn", which ironically are terms also used to describe "Jesus" in religious texts.

Is this the reason behind the Society of Jesus' worship of "Lucifer"? To what are they referring? Are the disciples of this society being deceived by unseen entities assuming the identity of such a character?

"Lucifer" was also the title of a monthly journal published by the Theosophical Society in London, England between 1887 and 1897, and its controversial title led to accusations of Blavatsky being a devil worshipper. However, she vehemently refuted such claims.

"There is no *devil* or the utterly depraved, as there are no Angels absolutely perfect, though there may be spirits of Light and of Darkness; thus LUCIFER – the spirit of Intellectual Enlightenment and Freedom of Thought – is metaphorically the guiding beacon, which helps man to find his way through the rocks and sandbanks of Life, for Lucifer is the LOGOS in his highest, and the "Adversary" in his lowest aspect – both of which are reflected in our Ego."[73] (p. 162)

"Our mind can either be our adversary (which is what the word "satan" literally means) or it can be the lightbearer (the Lucifer) of spiritual Truth to us, the knowledge of which brings about our liberations from the ignorance, including spiritual self-ignorance."[74]

Therefore, we could postulate that the worship of "Lucifer", may be the worship of knowledge. Yet the Society of Jesus could be led by the lower aspects, or desiring side of the mind and ego… in contrast with the Tibetan mystic traditions of using knowledge to serve others.

"Love" may then be interpreted as serving others while pursuing a spiritual path, and "evil", as serving the self in egotistical pursuits… an adversary to your spiritual path… or "satanic".

The concepts of "good" and "evil" are but opposite sides of a spectrum, formed by the dualistic nature of this realm, and the embodiment of these ideas into "angels" and "demons" stem from our belief in their existence.

The spiritual dimensions and the mechanisms of creation are well understood by those in power.

We have all seen the famous "Illuminati" "all seeing eye" pyramid symbol. It is littered throughout our lives in corporate logos, movies and literature. There seems to be no escape from its piercing gaze.

Where does this symbol originate? What is its true meaning? Why is it so important?

One suggestion is the pineal gland…

The pineal gland, or "third eye", is a light sensitive, pea sized endocrine gland centered in the brain, which produces melatonin and helps to regulate our circadian rhythms, and is shaped like a small pine cone… hence its name.

It has been well known and documented throughout our spiritual traditions as the link between the physical and the spiritual worlds.

A cross section of the area where it is located reveals the inspiration behind the Eye of Ra symbol.

It is said that activating the pineal gland will make it shine like a thousand suns, and empower you with a higher state of consciousness and understanding of life, a sense of calmness and clarity, as well as intuitive and psychic abilities.

Throughout thousands of years, the pineal gland has been known as the gateway to self-realization and spiritual enlightenment. It is undoubtably an important part of our physical being.

Many throughout history have claimed to be able to access different realms of existence through third eye activation and actually communicate with… and become possessed by… various spiritual entities.

All spiritual experiences, channelings, visions, possessions, and out of body experiences are apparently conducted through the third eye chakra.

Studies in Neuroscience however, show that when brain scans are performed with PET imaging equipment on a person that is meditating, a great deal of activity can be seen in the medial prefrontal cortex of the frontal lobe.

It is believed that part of its functionality is to have a calming effect on the mind and body, by down-regulating cortisol production, a hormone that is produced when a person is stressed, and may also play a vital role in helping to dampen the escalation of fear, which is managed by the Amygdala, a part of the brain that triggers the "fight or flight" response.

It was also discovered that meditation can shrink the Amygdala and increase the tolerances to stimulations that can trigger this "fight or flight" reaction, and create more emotional stability.

Brain scans have shown that another part of the frontal lobe called the Orbitofrontal Cortex, located just above the brow in the area where the third eye chakra is located, will light up during meditation. Signals are then sent to the mental, emotional, physiological and memory centers of the brain. A correlation can be made to mindful meditation practices which are meant to develop awareness to these same areas, and illuminate the third eye chakra.[75]

The third eye chakra may be linked to the frontal lobe, but may also be composed of a combination of the pineal gland and the frontal lobe. Its essence remains a mystery, yet may be kept a secret by those who do understand its power.

There has been a concerted effort amongst the keepers of knowledge to systematically extinguish this flame of awareness that we all possess, in order to build a class of uninformed and obedient servants, unaware of their true divinity.

How is this done?

In essence, our realities are created with our thoughts, therefore, by conditioning others to believe in a false reality, they will eventually manifest into this existence, a reality by design.

By hiding information and keeping the populace ignorant to their true nature and potential, while encouraging self-gratifying egotistical pursuits, you can keep the minds of the majority of the public confined to a world where their field of perception is very limited. Therefore, their attention is focused on basic survival needs and the small life pursuits of the material world, allowing them to be easily manipulated by those who possess the true knowledge of existence, and keep them trapped in this three-dimensional experience.

We become entangled in philosophical concepts that gain momentum through popularity, described as "pendulums" by Russian Quantum physicist, Vadim Zeland, in his book series titled "Reality Transurfing".[76]

The nature of pendulums is to attract as many followers as possible, in order to amplify its energy, and will set its adherents against other pendulums in order to justify its own self-righteous position.

Television programming and the media are powerful tools used to create such "pendulums", as it has the ability to reach an enormous population and provide tremendous momentum to clans, cliques, factions and cults that are focused on a variety of concepts such as sports, fashion, food, health, sickness, gaming, drinking, technology, music, movies, politics, religions and so on, thereby captivating and entrapping the minds of many, in hard to escape feedback loops of materialistically focused desires and subsistence.

We may understand the spiritual path of non-desire more closely when examining pendulums, as all pendulums are fed by physical and emotional needs which only exist in this dimensional reality. In contrast, a life devoted to love and service to others is a path of non-desire… a spiritual path that does not provide energy to pendulums and feed its necessity.

Less destructive pendulums are mainly used to keep the mind occupied, subdued and ignorant to spiritual realities, but the more emotionally charged ideologies found in political and religious doctrines may be used to very destructive ends to create conflict and war.

Well-known to those in power, is the paradox that trying to "fight" a pendulum actually feeds its energy.

Any who have opted to fight the system knows well the societal ostracization that one must endure when choosing to publicly express their alternative viewpoints, yet may often just be substituting one pendulum for another.

Alternative media personalities are put in place and promoted by the globalists with the purpose of energizing pendulums that will attract those who do not fall victim to the mainstream rhetoric, and persuade them into believing that they must fight the system through means that they have already established will empower their own objectives.

This well-funded "opposition" will also set a standard for others to follow, who will unknowingly set out to fight the system in the same unfruitful manner.

If they control the "opposition", they may ensure that no true knowledge emerges, and no energy is given to initiate any pendulums which would dissolve their own, which they have created to their own end.

Those whose minds are not satisfied with conventional interpretations and seek truth in alternative places are managed by this controlled opposition, which is designed to lead the aspirant down a path of anger and resentment towards the system and its perpetrators, therefore empowering the same pendulums, as their belief in this reality amplifies its existence. Only the few who have the potential to initiate and become leaders of pendulums which could attract enough followers to create a large enough movement to dissolve these pendulums of control, are sought after and eliminated.

The truth is in the details... and so I must point out a reckless oversight which I have found prevalent across the entire spectrum of new age teachings with few exceptions, of which I am also guilty of perpetrating in this book.

This carelessness comes in the form of neglecting the very foundation of the law of attraction teachings, and also brings to light the self-serving and ignorant aspects of human nature.

The fallacy of which I speak is the incessant finger pointing at the majority of the population, as being ignorant to whatever information is being transcribed by the teachers of these doctrines.

Most people have no idea… *Most people* are clueless… *Most people* don't understand…

This tendency is not only common practice amongst these spiritual teachers, but is subsequently adapted by their students, who then label *most people* in the same manner, in a form of self-aggrandizement. "I" am especially intelligent as "I" know something that *most people* don't know. Therefore "I" must be special.

This phenomenon seems to have become engrained into the fabric of society, as we curse our way through our daily lives, extending our criticisms to all whom we feel deserve such condemnation. No one who has dared express themselves on any platform is spared from the judging eyes of critics.

If one firmly believes that we create our reality with our thoughts, then should we not view *most people* as being enlightened with these spiritual truths?

These spiritual teachings espouse the virtues of non-judgementalism towards humanity, yet describing *most people* as being ignorant to these virtues is in itself a form of judgement.

If these spiritual gurus are intent on awakening humanity to spiritual wisdom, shouldn't they practice what they preach?

Although we can understand the necessity of proving a point, there is in most circumstances, no proof to be found in judgement. It would therefore be favorable to leave such mention ignored, as its intention has no basis in spirituality and can only befit egotism, as it is a form of vanity.

Realistically, no one can truly assess another's level of spiritual development, or their purpose in this lifetime. If you were to walk past Esther Hicks or Wayne Dyer at the market, having never encountered them in their work, you would not be able to recognize their level of spiritual maturity. They might to you, just be the jerk who bumped into you in aisle three. Unless of course it was an Indian guru with a long beard, wearing a robe and sandals as an entourage of devotees throw flower petals at his feet… at which point you may recognize this person's spiritual status. Yet these are but symbols, and only serve to portray an image which may or may not befit the person in question.

We might however, when considering the law of attraction, question the wisdom of being informed, or reading books such as this one. "What we don't know won't hurt us", should we say.

However, with lack of knowledge, one can be unconsciously led into destructive pendulums and feed their own serfdom.

In order to disempower such controlling forces, one must first be aware of its existence. Therefore, knowledge is instrumental, as it gives you the power to choose, consequently empowering yourself to live at new levels of personal and spiritual awareness and understanding.

Although a journey of exploration and self-realization can be met with loneliness, scorn, mockery, social ostracization and personal responsibility… which is cause enough for most to remain on the path of least resistance and accept the common narrative and social order… the results of this endeavor may uncover a life-altering potentiality.

I've always been a firm believer that anything is possible, and in this world of duality, there must be a solution to every problem. The answers however, might not correlate with expectation, or even exist in the realm of our comprehension.

Our willingness to open doors to the unknown and accept any possibility as the answer to a question, allows us to uncover the deepest truths.

I have watched millions of people protesting around the world, whether peacefully or violently, and noticed that these physical actions are never able to create the desired results. Our minds have been purposefully conditioned to accept the necessity of such actions through feelings of lack, desperation, anger and frustration, which will reflect an environment befitting those needs. Ironically, it is these very emotions that feed the situations that created the belief that such actions are necessary.

We must therefore consider that an understanding of the laws of creation, through self-awareness and mastery of the mind, may be the only path to effectively creating our desired life.

As the story progresses, the inevitability of disclosure persists and their scheme of disempowering the human race of its inherent creative abilities reveals itself. As more feel compelled to share their insights, the truth expands and becomes a force too great to be conquered by lies and deceit, as such manipulation tactics are part of the construct and are constrained within its boundaries. Awareness of one's true nature dissolves such limited egotistical concepts as it no longer feeds its necessity.

Through this process, the forces that seek to control, lose their very reason to exist. Our power is not outside of ourselves but within, at the seat of consciousness.

Chapter 11

EXPIRED TRUTH

I was having a conversation with the librarian who was in charge of the archives at the television station where I worked, and as he had always been firmly opposed to questioning the common narrative, that particular day I decided to ask him why he never took interest in the information I frequently presented to him. "Don't you want to know the truth?", I asked him.

His response was unexpected. "Maybe there is no truth", he stated.

What an absurd statement… I thought to myself… how can there be no truth?

Of course, "truth" can be relative to a person's knowledge and understanding, stem from the environment in which he/she was raised, and reflect their version of reality.

If I hold a cup in my hand, I can be honestly truthful in stating that I am holding a cup in my hand, and anyone being a witness to it, can attest to its truthfulness.

Yet truth may be subjective to the definitions of the words used to describe your truth. You may describe "holding" the cup as physically grasping it with your hand and being able to touch and move the cup to any desired position in space and time.

However, are you really touching this cup? From a physics point of view, there is actually no physical contact being made, as the atoms from your hand and the cup exert a repulsive force on each other which our brain translates as physical touch, yet is only sensing the electrical impulses caused by the magnetic repulsion effect.

We may also contemplate the existence of the cup. If we were to entertain the ancient mystic beliefs that our world is but an illusion, or a holographic construct, then the entirety of this existence may lie in a virtual landscape which we perceive as being real.

If you were playing a video game and your character held a sword in its hand, your observation would confirm this truth, yet the character in this game is simply a visual effect created through electronic circuits that are portraying an image on a screen which is composed of thousands of tiny pixels that when viewed with the human eye, mix together to form an image that you would perceive as a character wielding a sword, yet is simply an illusion created by tiny dots of colored lights.

Imagine that you had the ability to download your consciousness into the character in the video game and live inside this construct through this avatar, yet had no recollection or knowledge of yourself in the "real" world previous to the transfer. Your entire reality would be confined within the limits of the programming and whatever senses you were given that would allow you to interact with this electronic system environment. You may also be convinced of the truth that you are wielding a sword in your own hand, but the reality is that you are just being deceived by artificial senses, made to interact with your surroundings within the construct.

Therefore, in an illusory world, truth is relative to the observer.

"Nobody in this world possesses absolute truth. This is God's attribute alone. Relative truth is all we know." – *Mahatma Gandhi*

If we are indeed experiencing this reality through avatars we call our bodies, we must also explore our potential ability to alter and shape this artificial construct to our desires.

If our truth is relative to our own image of this reality, we can now better understand the holographic universe concept that our reality is simply a reflection of our imagination.

Seeking for truth therefore, may be a fruitless endeavor, when in fact, it is what you convince yourself of being true that holds more authority in creating the life which you desire to see manifest.

Knowledge therefore, may be viewed as the parameters from which is derived your truth. A broad knowledge base may permit you to create a more abundant and fulfilling life and allow you to gain more control over your fate. As your understanding of the world grows, your present truths will become expired and replaced with more meaningful truths, and consequently, result in a more inspired life.

If your path leads you towards spiritual teachings, your knowledge may grow into wisdom, where your truths could perhaps guide you towards developing a more selfless life in service to humanity. Such uplifting truths could also allow you to grow beyond this three-dimensional realm, into higher states of consciousness, as your truths would now be in alignment with higher dimensional realms of existence.

It's essential to recognize the importance of cultivating knowledge and awareness in your life, as ignorance results in dependence, which allows others to be able to easily manipulate you to serve their needs.

We are all familiar with the old adage that "ignorance is bliss", yet it is simply a reference to a child-like state of being that is free from personal accountability and responsibility, stem from a lack of knowledge. It is a trivial state of dependence and servitude.

The following example serves to demonstrate the significance of being aware and educated.

Imagine that there was a man who was purposely dumping toxins in your water supply. Being ignorant to his actions, all who were using this source of water for their needs were systematically being poisoned. You however, having the wisdom to question everything, deduced that there must be something wrong with the water, and upon careful investigation discovered the man's dirty deeds and exposed them to the public, at which point you were able to have the man arrested and stop the dumping of toxins in your water supply, and re-establish a clean source of water for everyone's needs.

Even though the townspeople were unaware of the toxins in their water, this unknown truth still permeated into their reality, as they were getting sick and dying from the effects of the poison. Being aware of such circumstances however, gives you the ability to choose, and take the necessary actions to secure your wellbeing.

This example holds true in all aspects of life, and knowledge therefore is crucial to our survival, as it allows our relative truths to become more sophisticated and defined, and can help guide us towards creating a better quality of life.

The information contained in this book is a compilation of certain truths I have come to discover throughout my life. You may choose to incorporate some of this knowledge into your relative truths and make decisions that may affect your life in a positive or negative manner.

Regardless of your circumstances, my truth tells me that you were led to read this book for your own specific reasons, in the same way that I was compelled to write it for my own personal reasons, and other purposes that I may never understand in this lifetime.

Our relative truths will all expire one day, and we will reconnect to the source in absolute truth, and appreciate the journey we all took to get there.

BIBLIOGRAPHY

1. Broadcasting Act (S.C. 1991, c. 11) - https://laws-lois.justice.gc.ca/eng/acts/b-9.01/page-1.html?wbdisable=true – Part III Canadian Broadcasting Corporation, Independence (5) 1991, c. 11, s. 46; 2014, c. 20 s. 366(E); 2023, c. 8. S. 29. – AGENT OF HER MAJESTY, Corporation an agent of Her Majesty 47 (1) – Property 47 (3)

2. "5 Crazy Facts About Lobbyists – Follow the Money #11", February 11, 2016 – https://www.youtube.com/watch?v=b4jdcdlquF0&t=363s – CC BY 3.0 https://creativecommons.org/licenses/by/3.0/

3. "Jack Abramoff: The lobbyist's playbook", Correspondent Lesley Stahl, CBS News, May 30, 2012 – https://www.cbsnews.com/news/jack-abramoff-the-lobbyists-playbook-30-05-2012/

4. "ANALYSIS: When a Congressman Becomes a Lobbyist, He Gets a 1,452% Raise (on Average)", by Lee Fang, March 14, 2012, Republic Report – https://www.republicreport.org/2012/make-it-rain-revolving-door/

5. "Only 2% to 10% of containers worldwide undergo inspection", updated January 10th, 2024 – https://www.icontainers.com/us/2016/11/11/friday-fun-fact-3-only-2-to-10-of-containers-are-inspected/

6. "China has acquired a global network of strategically vital ports", by Liz Sly and Julia Ledur, Nov. 6, 2024, The Washington Post – https://www.washingtonpost.com/world/interactive/2023/china-ports-trade-military-navy/

7. "China's Military Potential", Corporate Author; ARMY WAR COLL STRATEGIC STUDIES INST CARLISLE BARRACKS PA, Personal Author; Wortzel, Larry M., 1998-10-02, Accession Number: ADA358007 – https://apps.dtic.mil/sti/citations/ADA358007

8. "How China Could Shut Down America's Defenses", by Keith Johnson and Lara Seligman, June 11, 2019, Foreign Policy – https://foreignpolicy.com/2019/06/11/how-china-could-shut-down-americas-defenses-rare-earth/

9. "Soviet Subversion of the Free World Press", American Media, 1984 – YouTube link, "'Deception Was My Job' or 'Soviet Subversion of the Free World Press' (Complete Interview)", Kevin Heine – https://www.youtube.com/watch?v=jFfrWKHB1Gc

10. "91% of the time the better-financed candidate wins. Don't act surprised", by Wesley Lowery, April 14, 2014, The Washington Post – https://www.washingtonpost.com/news/the-fix/wp/2014/04/04/think-money-doesnt-matter-in-elections-this-chart-says-youre-wrong/

11. "Agreement Between Canada and the United States of America Relating to the Exchange of Information on Weather Modification Activities" – E103819 - CTS 1975 No. 11 – https://www.treaty-accord.gc.ca/text-texte.aspx?id=103819

12. "President John F. Kennedy – THE PRESIDENT AND THE PRESS: ADDRESS BEFORE THE AMERICAN NEWSPAPER PUBLISHERS ASSOCIATION", APRIL 27, 1961, Waldorf-Astoria Hotel, New York City, (PD) – https://www.jfklibrary.org/

13. "WTF? Two Prime Ministers, One speech", YouTube video uploaded by UndefeatedArmy09, August 22, 2009 – https://www.youtube.com/watch?v=nYfDTsjwE58

14. "Prediction #5: Plasma Formations in the Ancient Sky", David Talbott, Wallace Thornhill, et al, December 31, 2004 – https://www.thunderbolts.info/tpod/2004/arch/041231predictions-rock-art.htm

15. Modern Mechanix and Inventions, July edition, 1934 – PDF version – https://archive.org/details/sim_todays-homeowner-solutions_1934-07_12_3/page/118/mode/2up

16. "Gravity: It's only a Theory", by Ellery Schempp, National Center for Science Education, Volume 27, no. 5-6, September-December, 2007 – https://ncse.ngo/gravity-its-only-theory

17. "The guy who created the iPhone's Earth image explains why he needed to fake it", by David Yanofsky, March 27, 2014, Quartz – https://qz.com/192700/the-guy-who-created-iphones-earth-image-explains-why-he-needed-to-fake-it

18. "Robert Simmon – AKA Mr. Blue Marble", by Elizabeth M. Jarrell, June 12, 2012 – https://www.nasa.gov/people-of-nasa/goddard-people/robert-simmon-aka-mr-blue-marble/

19. "History of the Blue Marble", October 13, 2005, NASA – https://earthobservatory.nasa.gov/features/BlueMarble/BlueMarble_history.php

20. "'It is photoshop, but it has to be.' -NASA data visualizer", Robbglow, February, 2021 – https://www.youtube.com/watch?v=USd3lSHEEqA

21. "From a Million Miles Away, NASA Camera Shows Moon Crossing Face of Earth", by Karl B. Hille, August 5, 2015 – https://www.nasa.gov/solar-system/from-a-million-miles-away-nasa-camera-shows-moon-crossing-face-of-earth/

22. Gene Krantz, *Failure Is Not An Option*, 2000, Berkley Publishing – ISBN 0-425-17987-7

23. "Quantum Physics: David Bohm, Bohmian Wave Mechanics / Wholeness and the Implicate Order, The Holographic Universe", Geoff Haselhurst – https://www.spaceandmotion.com/Physics-David-Bohm-Holographic-Universe.htm

24. Micheal Talbot, *The Holographic Universe*, September, 2011, HarperCollins – ISBN 978-0062014108

25. "Aldous Huxley, Panel discussion, Ultimate revolution (The) Part I", March 20, 1962, Berkeley Language Center, (tape 157a) – https://digital.library.ucla.edu/catalog/ark:/21198/zz002b1414

26. Adolf Hitler, *Mein Kampf*, p. 197, 14th edition, (PD)

27. "335: Covid: There Is No Virus", Interview with Dr. Thomas Cowan, Wise Traditions Podcast, October 18, 2021, musixmatch.com – https://podcasts.musixmatch.com/podcast/wise-traditions-01h1ngdz40h1jbjfx464wgnv91/episode/335-covid-there-is-no-virus-01hjz7abr0hfsfxezz2ddq0kmw

28. "The causes of the corona crisis are clearly identified; Virologists who claim disease-causing viruses are science fraudsters and must be prosecuted", by Dr. Stefan Lanka, Wissenschafftplus, April, 2020 – https://wissenschafftplus.de/uploads/article/wissenschafftplus-virologists.pdf

29. "FOIs reveal that health/science institutions around the world (220 and counting!) have no record of SARS-COV-2 isolation/purification, anywhere, ever", Christine Massey – https://www.fluoridefreepeel.ca/fois-reveal-that-health-science-institutions-around-the-world-have-no-record-of-sars-cov-2-isolation-purification/

30. "Corporate Greed & Aids – Nobel Prize Recipient, Dr. Kary Mullis, Inventor of the PCR Test", November 16, 2023, originally from "Corporate Greed And Aids Santa Monica 12 July 1997" – https://www.bitchute.com/video/2pJISA0NRzW0/

31. "Luc Montagnier, Nobel-Winning Co-Discoverer of H.I.V., Dies at 89", by Randi Hutter Epstein, published Feb. 10, 2022, updated Feb. 11, 2022 – nytimes.com – https://www.nytimes.com/2022/02/10/science/luc-montagnier-dead.html

32. "Virus", by Howard Radcliffe, August 22, 2021, theresnothingnew.com – https://theresnothingnew.com/articles/virus/

33. "Heart May Not Be a Pump: Thomas Cowan on Cardiovascular Disease", High Intensity Health, Mike Mutzel – https://www.youtube.com/watch?v=ZFUomLdn9aQ&t=1690s

34. "The Velocity of Blood Flow in the Rabbit Aorta Studied with High-Speed Cinematography", D. A. McDonald, Department of Physiology, St Batholomew's Hospital Medical College, London, 1952 – https://www.ncbi.nlm.nih.gov/pmc/articles/PMC1392506/pdf/jphysiol01436-0045.pdf

35. "The Heart is Not a Pump – A Refutation of the Pressure Propulsion Premise of Heart Function", Ralph Marinelli, Branko Fuerst, Hoyte van der Zee, Andrew McGinn, William Marinelli, Journal of Anthroposophical Medicine, Volume 13, Spring 1996 https://www.aetherforce.energy/the-heart-is-not-a-pump-the-blood-moves-the-heart-not-vice-versa/

36. Woodrow Wilson, William Bayard Hale, *The New Freedom, A Call For the Emancipation of the Generous Energies of a People*, 1913, New York and Garden City Doubleday, Page & Company, The Project Glutenberg ebook version, January 26, 2005 [EBook #14811] – used under the terms of the Project Gutenberg License – https://www.gutenberg.org/files/14811/14811-h/14811-h.htm

37. M. Le Général Montholon, *Récits de la Captivité de L'Empereur Napoléon a Sainte-Hélène* – (*my translation: Recitation of the Captivity of Emperor Napoléon at Sainte-Hélène*), 1847, (PD), Paulin, Libraire-éditeur, Paris –
https://www.google.es/books/edition/R%C3%A9cits_de_la_Captivit%C3%A9_de_l_Empereur_N/y7gPAAAAQAAJ?gbpv=1

Original citation in French:

"Mais une société religieuse bien dangereuse et qui jamais n'aurait été admise sur les terres de l'Empire, c'est la société de Jésus. Sa doctrine est subversive de tous principes monarchiques. Le général des jésuites veut être le souverain maître, le souverain dans le souverain. Partout où les jésuites sont admis il leur faut le pourvoir à tout prix. Leur société est dominatrice par nature, et dès lors elle est ennemie et ennemie irréconciliable de tout ce qui est pouvoir. Toute action, tout crime, quelque atroce qu'il soit, est une oeuvre méritoire s'il est commis dans l'intérêt de la société de Jésus ou par ordre du général des jésuites."

38. Thomas M. Harris, Late Brigadier General, U.S.V., *Rome's Responsibility for the Assassination of Abraham Lincoln*, 1897, The Williams Publishing Company, Pittsburg, (PD)
https://ia800308.us.archive.org/25/items/romesrespons3431harr/romesrespons3431harr.pdf

39. "Thomas Woods: The Catholic Church built Western civilization", by Pioneer Press, Published: December 26, 2011 | UPDATED: November 13, 2015 –
https://www.twincities.com/2011/12/26/thomas-woods-the-catholic-church-built-western-civilization/

40. Thomas E. Woods, Jr., Ph.D., *How the Catholic Church Build Western Civilization*, 2005, Regnery Publishing Inc, Wahington, DC – ISBN 0-89526-038-7

41. Jonothan Wright, *God's Soldiers: Adventure, Politics, Intrigue, and Power--A History of the Jesuits*, 2005, publisher; Image – ISBN 978-0385500807

42. "Address to the 42d Session of the United Nations General Assembly in New York, New York", September 21, 1987, Ronald Reagan Presidential Library and Museum – https://www.reaganlibrary.gov/archives/speech/address-42d-session-united-nations-general-assembly-new-york-new-york

43. "I'd go to the moon, but we don't have that technology anymore - NASA Astronaut Don Pettit", The Earth Question – https://www.youtube.com/watch?v=16MMZJlp_0Y

44. "Moon landing tapes got erased, NASA admits", by Maggie Fox, Reuters, July 16, 2009 – https://www.reuters.com/article/uk-nasa-tapes-sb/moon-landing-tapes-got-erased-nasa-admits-idUKTRE56F5RV20090716/

45. "National Cultural Development Under Communism", June, 1957, Approved for Release 1999/08/24 : CIA-RDP78-02771R000200090002-6 – https://pendulumsofpower.com/wp-content/uploads/2024/01/CIA-RDP78-02771R000200090002-6-Tartaria-reference.pdf

46. "Faith Fights Communism: The United States and Islam in Saudi Arabi During the Cold War", thesis submitted by Robert M. Morrison, University of North Carolina, 2009 – http://dl.uncw.edu/Etd/2009-1/morrisonr/robertmorrison.pdf

47. "Gateway City, Documents on the City of Winnipeg 1873-1913", by Alan F.J. Artibise, The Manitoba Record Society Publications Volume V, 1979

48. "Manitoba College in Pictures", University of Winnipeg – https://www.uwinnipeg.ca/manitoba-college-150/slideshow.html

49. "A History of Brick Manufacturing in Manitoba, 1860-1990", David Butterfield, 2018 – A History of Brick Manufacturing PDF

50. "Winnipeg's Early Days", W. J. Healy, 1927, Stovel Company Limited – http://www.mb1870.org/localhistory/134%20-%20Healy,%20Winnipeg's%20Early%20Days.pdf

51. Records and archives for the Manitoba Free Press, Fiftieth Anniversary Number, Winnipeg, November 9, 1922, p. 22, (PD) – https://www.flickr.com/photos/manitobamaps/2361897059/

52. "An Introduction to Manitoba's Architectural History", Heritage Manitoba, – https://heritagemanitoba.ca/images/pdfs/An_Introduction_to_MB_Architectural_History_Heritage_MB.pdf

53. "Building a Nation" – https://cpconnectingcanada.ca/our-history/

54. "Building Through The Prairies", by Craig Baird, September 23, 2021, Canadian History Ehx – https://canadaehx.com/2021/09/23/building-through-the-prairies/

55. "The Rail, From Sea to Sea", Canadian Museum of History – https://cpconnectingcanada.ca/our-history/

56. "Tunneling Into History: The Amy Street Steam Heating Plant", Heritage Winnipeg Blog, December 22, 2022 – https://heritagewinnipeg.com/blogs/tunneling-into-history-the-amy-street-steam-heating-plant/

57. Claude Valla, *La France sous les bombes américaines,* 2008, publisher; Encre – ISBN 13: 9782911202445 – Synopsis can be read here: https://www.abebooks.co.uk/9782911202445/France-bombes-am%C3%A9ricaines-French-Edition-2911202449/plp

58. "Photography, What it Is and How It Is Done", Illinois College of Photography, 1905-1906, (PD) – https://archive.org/details/illinoiscollegeo00illi/page/6/mode/2up

59. Official Guide to the World's Columbian Exposition, In the City of Chicago, State of Illinois, May 1 to October 26, 1893 – https://archive.org/details/officialguidetow00flin/page/n7/mode/2up?view=theater

60. "The World's Columbian Exposition: Idea, Experience, Aftermath", Julie K. Rose, 1993 – https://web.archive.org/web/20180719054910/https://libraet d.lib.virginia.edu/downloads/g158bh33j?filename=1_Rose_Jul ie_1996_MA.pdf

61. David F. Burg, *Chicago's White City of 1893*, 1976, University Press of Kentucky – ISBN 978-0-8131-0140-8

62. "From the Hyde Park Historical Society newsletter -- *The Big Wheel* Spring 2000", by Patrick Meehan – https://web.archive.org/web/20130118143455/http:/www.hy deparkhistory.org/newsletter.html

63. "The 1893 Chicago World's Columbian Exposition Observation (Ferris) Wheel", compiled by Dr. Neil Gale, Ph.D., January 11, 2017 – https://drloihjournal.blogspot.com/2017/01/1893-worlds-columbian-exposition.html

64. "Frederick Law Olmsted's 1893 Report to the American Institute of Architects", The American Architect and Building News, September 9, 1893, Vol. XLI, No. 924

65. "Interview with Nikola Tesla – Making Your Imagination Work For You", M.K. Wisehart, The American Magazine, April, 1921, (PD)

66. Unclassified FBI document – MEMORANDUM FOR MR. FOXWORTH, January 9, 1943, (PD) – https://vault.fbi.gov/nikola-tesla/Nikola%20Tesla%20Part%2003%20of%2003

67. "Tesla Slept Here", by Marc Singer, The New Yorker, January, 2008 – https://www.newyorker.com/magazine/2008/01/14/tesla-slept-here

68. "New Yorker Hotel", New World Encyclopedia – CC-BY-SA – https://creativecommons.org/licenses/by-sa/3.0/ - https://www.newworldencyclopedia.org/entry/New_Yorker_Hotel#External_links

69. "Experiment confirms quantum theory weirdness", Associate Professor Andrew Truscott from the ANU Research School of Physics and Engineering, Australian National University – https://health.anu.edu.au/news-events/news/experiment-confirms-quantum-theory-weirdness

70. "The Whitewashing of Black Magic", blavatskytheosophy.com – https://blavatskytheosophy.com/the-whitewashing-of-black-magic/

71. "The Danger and Deception of Channeling", blavatskytheosophy.com – https://blavatskytheosophy.com/the-danger-and-deception-of-channelling/

72. "Excerpt from Bob Dylan's 60 Minutes Interview - The Chief Commander", Sage of Quay – https://www.youtube.com/watch?v=lpfRiryELFM

73. Blavatsky, H. P., *The Secret Doctrine,* (Vol. 2), 1888, The Theosophical Publishing Company Limited, London, – ISBN 978-1-55700-228-0

74. "Lucifer the Lightbringer", blavatskytheosophy.com –
https://blavatskytheosophy.com/lucifer-the-lightbringer/

75. "Body Mind Psychotherapist", Energetics Institute, Perth,
West Australia, by Richard Boyd, 2011 – re-posted as: "The
Scientific Basis For the Spiritual Concept of the Third Eye", by
Consciousreminder, April, 2017 –
https://consciousreminder.com/2017/04/12/scientific-basis-spiritual-concept-third-eye/

76. Vadim Zeland, *Reality Transurfing 1. The Space of Variations*,
translated by Natasha Micharina, 2008, O-Books – ISBN 978 1
84694 122 1

GLOSSARY OF TERMS

Audio console
A device that is used to process various sound sources and mix them down to a single mono or stereo output.

Character generator
A device, or computer that is used to generate titles and fonts that appears on screen.

Cut
An edit point in visual and audio material editing. Derived from the physical cutting and pasting method of editing film and audio tape. The process of transitioning from one source to another on a live broadcast.

EFP
Electronic Field Production. The process of gathering video and audio material, to subsequently be edited into various television productions.

ENG
Electronic News Gathering. The process of gathering video and audio material for the purpose of producing news items on a live news program.

Font Operator
Person operating a character generator

Master Control
The main distribution hub of all material being aired by a television broadcaster.

Mic

A microphone. Pronounced "mike". A device used to transform physical sound into an electronic signal.

Monitor

A technological device resembling a television set used to monitor visual material.

PA

Production Assistant. A control room assistant to the director whose main task is to clock every element of a live news broadcast to the last second and ensure proper cues and compliance to the established timeline of the broadcast.

PA System

Public Address System. An audio system composed of speakers, amplifiers, cables and microphones, used to boost the audio signal in larger settings where communication requires amplification.

Remote

An on-location reporting crew.

Shot

The visual representation of a camera's settings and position.

Streeter

Interviews that are conducted on the street with pedestrians regarding various subjects of interest.

Studio Assistant

An in-studio assistant that directs the studio cameramen and on camera personalities, facilitates communication with the control room, and helps with technical issues.

Switcher

A device used to mix the video content aired on a television program. Also used to identify the technician who works with a switcher.

Teleprompter

A device used in conjunction with a visual display which is placed in front of the camera to assist on air personalities with reading their texts, so as to avoid having to constantly look down at their sheets, enabling them to read text while retaining eye contact with the camera lens.

Telex

A partially hidden in-ear device used to facilitate communication between members of the production crew.

Television Technician

A broad term used to describe a person who is an audio engineer, cameraman, switcher, video/audio editor, electrical engineer, or any person who is in charge of any technical aspect of a television production.

VJ

Video Jockey. A journalist that independently researches, writes, shoots and edits his/her own items.

VO

Voice Over. A visual element of a news broadcast, whereas the host will be reading a text live on air, while related visual material is being shown on the screen.

VTR

Video Tape Recorder

Acknowledgements

Behind the scenes of the media and entertainment industries, is a mostly unseen world of technicians, engineers, stage hands, riggers, writers, editors, journalists, directors, producers and more, functioning as a whole to deliver a world class product to their audience.

The programs we watch on our television screens, the shows and concerts we enjoy, are but the end results of the tremendous efforts of these amazingly skilled and dedicated professionals, with whom I've had the great honor and pleasure of working with throughout my career, and which I hold in great regard.

Thank you for your work, your dedication, and your friendship.